LOVE AND SEX
AFTER 40

Also by Robert N. Butler, M.D., and Myrna I. Lewis, A.C.S.W.

AGING AND MENTAL HEALTH: Positive Psychosocial and Biomedical Approaches (Third Edition)
SEX AFTER SIXTY: A Guide for Men and Women for Their Later Years

Also by Robert N. Butler, M.D.

WHY SURVIVE? Being Old in America
HUMAN AGING (co-author)

PREFACE

After writing a book called *Sex After Sixty* over ten years ago, we became increasingly aware that the topics we had discussed—worries about body changes with age, fears about impotence and loss of sexual attractiveness, anxieties about social acceptance in a culture that idealizes youth, relationship problems over time, and other issues—were as much a concern for the middle-aged as for those who were older. We therefore put ourselves the task of revising and enlarging our original book to include midlife as well. We ended by writing what is essentially a new book.

Our society is in the midst of a longevity revolution. Prehistoric people lived an estimated eighteen years. The average early Greek and Roman life expectancy was thirty-three years. And U.S. life expectancy at the turn of the twentieth century was only forty-seven years. Since that time we have gained an astounding twenty-five years of average life expectancy.

Only during the last several centuries did a sufficient number of people live long enough lives to compel a popular interest in different life stages—youth, middle age, and old age—each with its own characteristics. The study of these stages did not seriously begin until well into the present century, when basic life cycle issues were identified and personality development and growth over time studied. Adolescents struggle with autonomy and independence; the middle-aged evaluate and often redirect their values, their work, and their emotional commitments; and psychologically healthy older persons tend to concentrate on assessing and nurturing their own personality growth and their relationships with others, as well as appreciating and enjoying the elemental pleasures of life.

As people live longer there is increased interest and speculation about what happens to sexuality over time. We present here the latest medical and scientific evidence about the effects of stress, illness, disability, drugs, and certain surgeries on sexuality, plus the significance of what is known about the aging process itself. We address the problems of finding professional help for sexual problems and learning to communicate optimally with doctors and other professionals. Psychological issues of the middle and later years and problems with relationships are discussed as well. We have written this book for the general public, and for doctors, psychotherapists, nurses, social workers, counselors, and other health care providers to refer to their clientele. Our conviction is that sexual desires, pleasure, and performance can be lifelong and that relationships can grow and thrive throughout a lifetime.

What has changed in the ten years since we originally wrote on this subject?

- There has been significant improvement in the medical diagnosis of sexual problems; in surgical procedures that in the past inadvertently damaged sexual functioning; in the administration of drugs, to avoid adverse sexual side effects; and in the treatment of sexual problems caused by both acute and chronic illness and disability.
- Professionals working with both the psychological and the physical aspects of sexuality have taken a growing interest in the issues of the middle and later years. The chances of finding a knowledgeable physician, sex counselor, or psychotherapist are therefore greater than they were ten years ago.
- Midlife is increasingly seen as a time with sexual issues and concerns of its own as well as a time to develop health habits and

psychological skills that will prevent problems later on. The middle years are also optimal for the early diagnosis and treatment of sexual problems before they grow larger or become chronic.

- A dramatic change over the last few years has been the increasing acceptance by the public, by the professions, and by older people themselves of the importance of sexuality in later life. Radio, television, movies, and the press have begun to deal seriously with the topic. Older people are feeling freer to talk about sex and to seek medical and psychological help when they have problems. Even nursing homes are beginning to address the subject and offer training programs for staff members.

- The special situation of midlife and older women as a result of the shorter life expectancy of men, greater physical infirmity in men already in late middle age, and the social practice of men pairing off with women some years younger than themselves is starting to be explored. Medical research is moving in the direction of studying specifically why women live so much longer and what can be learned from them to help men. The study of the "killer diseases" like heart disease that affect men earlier and differently than women is progressing. The unequal social treatment of women as they grow older is being challenged by a number of individuals as well as women's, private, and governmental organizations. Women themselves are assuming prerogatives formerly reserved for males, such as dating younger partners and taking the initiative in social situations.

These changes are encouraging signs that sex after forty is a dynamic, evolving subject, worthy of interest and exploration. We hope our book will contribute to that evolution.

ACKNOWLEDGMENTS

A number of colleagues in the medical field have read portions or the entirety of this book in manuscript and we want to acknowledge gratefully their help: Dr. Charles Herrara, geriatrician/internist; Dr. Diane Meier, geriatrician/internist; Dr. Raul Schiavi, psychiatrist; Dr. Patricia Schreiner-Engel, psychologist; and Dr. Arnold Melman, urologist. All are associated with the Mount Sinai School of Medicine.

We especially thank Carol Cohen, our editor at Harper & Row, for her constructive and sensitive guidance and criticism.

LOVE AND SEX
AFTER 40

1

INTRODUCTION: FEARS OF THE FORTIES AND STEREOTYPES OF THE SIXTIES

FACING THE FORTIES

The fear of losing one's sexual ability or physical attractiveness is a major anxiety that begins to confront many people in their forties. These fears express themselves differently in men than in women, but the experience of anxiety is common to both sexes.

One of the most important emotional issues for men in their forties is the fear of sexual impotence or of inability to perform. Men are victims of a lifelong excessive emphasis on physical performance. Masculinity is equated with physical prowess. Men judge themselves and are judged by comparing the frequency and potency of their sexual performance with that of younger men, and when measured by these standards, which are essentially athletic, middle-aged and especially older men are naturally at a disadvantage. Unfortunately, these comparisons seldom place any value on experience and on the quality of sex for themselves and their partners.

The first sign of any change may produce panic: "Lately I've

1

been troubled by the fact that I seem to take longer to have a good erection. Is something wrong? Am I becoming impotent? Will I be able to have a firm erection as I get older? Will sex be as pleasurable as when I was younger? Will my partner think I am inadequate?" In addition to anxiety over performance, men who do not know about the *normal* physiological changes in sexual functioning that begin around the age of forty may believe falsely that they are becoming impotent.

The sex organs are a sensitive barometer of feelings and quickly reflect a man's state of mind. Fear and anxiety will almost inevitably cause a man to lose an erection or fail to have one in the first place. Fears of impotence can cause impotence. Relaxation, freedom from pressure, and accurate information about normal sexual functioning in the middle years are antidotes to fear-induced impotence.

The actual experience of impotence occurs occasionally in nearly all men, of all ages (yes, even teenagers), for a variety of reasons—among them fatigue, tension, boredom, guilt, depression, work and family pressures, illness, and excessive drinking. In most cases potency returns by itself without specific treatment as soon as the responsible physical or emotional causes are understood and removed or modified. Sudden and isolated attacks of impotence are primarily the result of some unusual stress, and typically abate when the stress is relieved. If problems continue for any considerable period of time, information and reassurance from a doctor or a professional counselor may be all that is needed. However, if the impotence persists, comprehensive medical evaluation and treatment as well as psychotherapy and/or sexual counseling may be required.

Women are under less pressure to "perform" sexually, but they are subject to an equally relentless expectation—the pressure to remain forever young-looking and "sexually attractive." As women reach their forties, they may become anxious and even frantic in the belief that they are no longer desirable. Growing older means a loss of self-esteem and social value. Our culture reinforces these notions at every turn, with a youth-oriented ideal of beauty that lacks the sophistication to include character, intelligence, expressiveness, knowledge, achievement, warmth, style, and social skills—those personal traits that make each woman unique and are found at any age.

Even more profound emotional and sexual dilemmas for

women revolve around the possibility of finding themselves—widowed, divorced, or separated—without partners, beginning in midlife and accelerating with each decade that follows. A current fact of life in the United States and throughout the industrialized world is that there are more women than men. By age twenty-five there are already more girls surviving than boys, and by age eighty-five and older, the proportions are two and one half women for every man. In 1984 there were 23.4 million women and 21.4 million men aged forty-five to sixty-four in the United States. But at age sixty-five and older, the proportions were 16.7 million women and only 11.3 million men. Not only are there more women than men, but there is also a much higher proportion of women than men without partners. Of the 16.7 million older women, 39.7 percent are married, 50.5 percent are widows, an additional 4.2 percent are divorced, and 5.6 percent never married, compared to men, who are 77.8 percent married, 14.0 percent widowed, 3.1 percent divorced, and 5.0 percent never married.

The major reason for these differences in partner availability is that females have had a greater life expectancy than males since at least the turn of the twentieth century, and the difference has been increasing. In 1983 life expectancy at birth was 78.1 for females and 71.0 for males. A second factor is that women tend to marry men who are three to four years older than themselves, further reducing the available numbers of men for older women. Finally, a significant proportion of men marry women who are substantially younger (up to fifteen or more years) than themselves during second or third marriages, bypassing their own age group altogether.

Anticipating the possible loss of a partner as well as the negative attitudes toward older women and other consequences of growing older as females today, women may find the first signs of gray hair and wrinkles in their late thirties and their forties to be uneasy portents of things to come. It is inaccurate to dismiss such apprehension as female vanity. Women could adjust much more comfortably to the physical changes of mid and later life if the life expectancy of men and women were more equal and if women were not stigmatized by the belief that only the young are beautiful or desirable.

It is no coincidence that sexual problems between partners often begin in the middle years, when people are preoccupied with earning a living, advancing their careers, and carrying out responsibilities for both young and older members of their family. Emotional and physical fatigue, overwork, boredom, and worries about family or finances can all affect sexuality. Sexual problems are often one of the first symptoms of psychological stresses such as depression, disappointment, sadness, grief, resentment, anger, and anxiety. Conflict with one's partner may be either the cause or a result of these stresses when there often is too little time left to pay attention to and develop one's personal relationships, while busyness can mask the lack of communication between partners. Role changes due to shifts over time in the emotional equilibrium between partners may bring added confusion. Divorce and widowhood grow in frequency in the middle and later years.

The normal physical and sexual changes that occur with growing older may cause distress in a relationship, particularly if they are unexpected or misunderstood. Illnesses, especially those of a more chronic nature, can interfere with sexuality, often unnecessarily. Much depends on knowing what to expect and how to handle it, beginning already in the middle years. Throughout this book we will focus on what is now known about sexuality in middle age, as well as what can be done in midlife to prevent or decrease sexual difficulties in the later years.

STEREOTYPING AFTER SIXTY

Love and sex past sixty, when acknowledged at all, are often patronizingly thought of as "cute" or "sweet," like the puppy love of teenagers. It is even more likely that they will be ridiculed—the subject of jokes that have undercurrents of disdain and apprehensiveness at the prospect of growing older. Mother-in-law jokes and none-too-flattering stories follow women from middle age into old age. Older women are still often depicted in fairy tales, advertisements, and cartoons as "biddies" and "hags." Men don't escape, either. Our language is full of such telltale phrases as "dirty old men," "old fools," or "old goats," with sexual connotations. Most of this "humor" implies the impotence of older men and the ugliness of older women.

A mythology fed by misinformation surrounds late-life sexuality. The presumption is that sexual desire automatically ebbs with age—that it begins to decline when one is in one's forties, proceeds relentlessly downward (you are "losing it"), and eventually hits bottom (you are "over the hill") at some time between sixty and sixty-five. Thus a woman over seventy or eighty who shows an evident, perhaps even a lusty, interest in sex is often asssumed to be suffering from emotional problems. If she is obviously in her right mind and yet sexually active, she runs the risk of being considered pathetic or "clinging to lost youth." As for men, what is viewed as lustiness in the young is frequently called lechery in the old. Even an older man's show of genuine affection toward children other than his own family risks being greeted with suspicion, as though automatically sexually tinged.

Why is our society so negative about sex in later life and about older people in general? Much of this attitude is an outgrowth of fears of growing old and dying, and it has given rise to the prejudice we call *ageism*, which is systematic discrimination against people because they are old, just as racism and sexism discriminate for reasons of skin color and gender. As far as sexuality is concerned, ageism is largely a matter of desexualization in its ultimate form: If you are older, you're finished.

These attitudes are relatively recent, since at the turn of the century, when the average life expectancy was forty-seven years, few people lived to old age and fewer still were healthy enough to be sexually active. But today life expectancy averages seventy-four years and we have a large population of relatively healthy people over sixty-five.

Cultural negativism toward the old and idealization of youthful physical appearance and performance can cause uncertainty and confusion for older people. They may experience anxiety about physical changes, feel the need to apologize for themselves, or become shy about their bodies. Such "body anxiety" may be more deeply felt by certain older people, leading to an exaggerated belief that they are ugly and undesirable. Others look into the mirror and insist that what they see "is not the real me." Some actually begin to act a role, a stereotyped, desexualized image of what an older person *should* be. The result is demoralization and giving up. Some decide that sexual ability is gone; the person arbitrarily declares himself or herself to be sexually incapacitated. Angry or obstinate refusal to discuss the issue with the partner or to consider possible remedies is typical in these instances.

Sometimes older people respond to their own sexual and social situation with anger and hostility toward those who are younger. One hears bitter threats, such as, "You'll see what it's like when *you're* old," or "Wait until you reach *my* age." There may also be self-righteous criticism of the sexuality of their own contemporaries as well as of the young.

Misinformation or out-of-date information may be part of the picture. For example, many men and women in their sixties and older grew up being told that "nice" women were not interested in sex and perhaps even found it distasteful. Passivity, resignation, and acceptance of male initiative were the ideal female patterns; it was "loose" women who gave themselves to the pleasures of sex or sought it. These attitudes are not always easy to dismiss simply because the younger generation no longer share them or let their lives be ruled by them.

A surprising number of older men and women also think that they can "wear themselves out" sexually. One specific belief is that too much sexual activity reduces potency and lowers semen "reserves." As late as 1937, a sex hygiene manual from the U.S. Public Health Service was warning youths not to "waste vital fluids." The 1945 edition of the *Boy Scout Manual* repeated this message, mainly to discourage masturbation.

Masturbation itself was the subject of many anxious pronouncements not so many years ago. In the late nineteenth and early twentieth centuries, children were warned that masturbation could cause feeblemindedness or madness; it could "use up the life juices," weaken the body, and shorten the life span. Nervousness, distractability, and a high-strung personality were considered clues to secret self-stimulation. Mechanical devices were designed to prevent children from masturbating at night, and surgery to remove the clitoris from little girls who masturbated "excessively" was a part of pediatric practice in some parts of the United States well into the twentieth century. It is therefore interesting today that masturbation is not only considered a normal form of sexual expression; it is also recommended as a way of preserving sexual capacity during periods when a partner may not be available, as is discussed later in this book.

FOR THOSE NOT INTERESTED IN SEX

We have been sketching a number of the ways—positive and negative—in which individuals and society react to sex. But what if people are not particularly interested in sex, as is true with a proportion of the population? We want to emphasize that sexual disinterest or abstinence is a matter of concern only when it is personally troubling or causes problems in relating to others. Evidence indicates that it is quite possible to live a satisfying and productive life without sex. Certain people never were significantly interested in sex even as young people, whether because of biological makeup or, more often, as a result of social conditioning. Others have found sex to be a long-standing focus of emotional conflict, resulting from or causing difficult relations with their partners. For them and their partners, the opportunity to discontinue sex under any socially acceptable guise can be a great relief. There are others who have simply grown tired of sex. It may have been shared with the same partner in a routine manner for a number of years, while both partners increasingly occupied themselves by developing satisfying nonsexual activities. Other people may have stopped sex because of disabilities or serious illnesses, and abstinence has developed into a comfortable habit. Sometimes an individual has made a deliberate decision to share sex only with a particular partner, and when illness or death intervenes, sex ends. Other people view sex only for procreation, not pleasure, so sex ends with the completion of childbearing or with the menopause.

Self-imposed abstinence from sex may also be the continuation of a lifelong habit. This can often be traced back to frightening early experiences or to feelings that sex is forbidden and dangerous, and the avoidance of sex altogether may provide an adjustment that works reasonably well. Abstinence is sometimes chosen for religious reasons as well.

We have written this book as a guide for people over forty who *are* interested in sex but may have apprehensions, fears, and even specific physical and emotional problems that interfere with sexual expression. We have gathered together the available research evidence and combined it with our own clinical experience to address the concerns that are most commonly expressed. It is our conviction that sexuality is an important part of the whole of life for many and perhaps the majority of people, and that we ought to take seriously the challenge of preserving and even improving on it as we reach the middle and later years.

PART ONE
PHYSICAL ISSUES

2

NORMAL PHYSICAL CHANGES IN SEXUALITY WITH AGE

What happens to your body sexually in the middle and later years? There are significant changes in the physical and physiological aspects of sex with age, but in the absence of disease or adverse drug effects, such changes do not usually cause sexual problems.

The act of sex is complex, encompassing the body, the mind, and the emotions. It involves the nervous system and the hormones as well as specific organs of the body. All participate in the sexual response cycle, which includes sexual desire, followed by the excitement or erotic arousal phase; the orgasmic or climax phase; and the resolution or recovery phase. Essentially the same phases hold true for both men and women.

People are stimulated sexually in a number of ways—through sight, smell, touch, thoughts, and feelings. The pelvic area reacts. Muscle tension and congestion (filling of the blood vessels) occur, especially in the sexual or genital organs. The sex hormones that play an active role in this responsiveness are chemically steroids, produced in the adrenal glands of both men and women, as well as

in the ovaries of women and the testes of men. They are discharged directly into the bloodstream, are carried to various organs, and affect the functioning of these organs. Estrogen, one of the active female hormones, has a profound effect on the development and functioning of the female sex organs. Androgen, the primary male hormone, appears to influence sexual desire in both men and women (women have small amounts of androgen), as well as sexual development and performance in men. Hormone levels are influenced by the body's master gland, the pituitary, in the brain. It is indeed a very complex system.

WOMEN

PREMENOPAUSAL PHYSICAL CAPACITY

From age forty until menopause begins, women may find themselves physically at full and relatively problem-free sexual capacity. Many have become well acquainted with and adapted to their personal sexual cycles and have gained the experience necessary to enhance their own response and that of their partners. Those who are experiencing difficulties will find that competent help is available to assist them with their problems.

MENOPAUSAL PHYSICAL CHANGES

Most of the sexual changes in women can be directly traced to the decline of female hormones, especially estrogen, before, during, and after menopause. Menopause, also called the "change of life" or "climacteric," is a physiological process which continues for several years, anywhere between ages thirty-five and fifty-five, but usually between forty-five and fifty, with fluctuations in estrogen levels from normal to near zero. Its most conspicuous sign is the cessation of menstruation.

The median age of the completion of menopause, fifty or fifty-one years, has remained unchanged since medieval times. In contrast, the median age for the beginning of menstruation has dropped an average of three to four months every ten years for the last one hundred years and is now twelve years and nine months. The age

of menopause is remarkably unaffected by any factors (socioeconomic status, age of onset of menstruation, race, size, and so forth) other than smoking. The latter appears to produce an earlier menopause in some women.

Menopause is a rich source of superstitions. Many believe the loss of sexual desire and attractiveness, the inevitability of depression, the occurrence of severe physical symptoms, masculinization, and even insanity are inevitable consequences. Actually, 60 percent of all women experience no remarkable physical or emotional symptoms with menopause, and of those who do, most have only minimal to moderate physical problems. Symptoms resulting from hormonal imbalance may include hot flashes, headaches and neckaches, excessive fatigue, and feelings of emotional instability. None of these are inevitable, and when they do occur, they often can be greatly alleviated or sometimes entirely relieved by various treatments. Life stresses can precipitate or exacerbate menopausal symptoms, and psychological counseling can be helpful under these circumstances. Even left untreated, certain menopausal symptoms subside spontaneously in time.

Fears surrounding menopause appear to be stronger in younger premenopausal women than in women who have actually completed menopause, according to studies by Bernice Neugarten at the University of Chicago. This would suggest that the discomfort and disadvantages of menopause are exaggerated in the minds of women who have not personally experienced them.

The sleep deprivation that can result from hot flashes may lead secondarily to emotional consequences. But there are no other patterns of mental performance, mood, or psychological states that have been associated with menopause or estrogen deprivation, such as a high incidence of new and distinctive mental illness. However, menopause does mark a psychological time of transition that may require support and guidance.

The menopause "hot flash" or "flush" is the most common symptom of menopause. Up to 80 percent of women have hot flashes and about 25 percent of women seek medical help for the discomfort. Hot flashes are a sensation of warmth and heat, followed by profuse sweating in the upper body. The frequency, duration and intensity of hot flashes varies considerably. These symptoms often last at least a year and often for three to four years or more. A few

women report hot flashes as late as their eighties. (The approximately 5 percent of American women who experience severe premenstrual symptoms [PMS] earlier in life may find these symptoms exacerbate around the menopause period.) Some women report that sexual activity can bring on a hot flash just prior to orgasm, resulting in a profuse sweat and a loss of the orgasm. Such symptoms usually disappear as hot flashes resolve themselves over time or with treatment.

The precise cause of hot flashes remains unclear. Increased levels or pulses of hormones influenced by decreasing levels of estrogen are one possible explanation; the higher central nervous systems such as the hypothalamus in the brain appears to be involved. It is speculated that the central heat regulator of the body misperceives the body as overheating and activates the heat loss mechanism of the hot flash. Studies of the hot flash are complicated by the fact the animals do not seem to experience them; studies at the National Institutes of Health and other research centers are therefore confined to human subjects.

The Women's Association for Research in Menopause (W.A.R.M.) raises funds for research on menopausal problems, promotes public education on the subject, and facilitates the formation of a national network of support groups. W.A.R.M. is located at Parkeast Executive Center, 128 East 56th Street, New York, N.Y. 10022.

During or, more usually, following menopause, large numbers of women begin to show other signs of estrogen or sex steroid losses, which can affect their sexual functioning. Vaginal lubrication—the physiological equivalent of the male erection—produced by congestion of the blood vessels in the vaginal wall, begins to take longer. This seems to be due both to the loss of estrogen necessary for its production and to changes in the structure of the vaginal wall, through which the secretions ooze. When this vaginal dryness occurs, intercourse may feel scratchy, rough, and eventually painful. However, even without adequate self-produced lubrication, women report that they are able to have orgasms, especially if they use a substitute lubrication, like K-Y jelly, Today, or Lubafax. Thus, while self-lubrication is ordinarily an indication of physiological sexual arousal, its absence does not indicate a lack of emotional sexual excitement nor does it preclude orgasm.

Typically, the lining of the vagina begins to thin and becomes easily irritated, leading to pain and perhaps cracking and bleeding during and after intercourse. Such pain (dyspareunia) occurs especially if intercourse is lengthy or follows a long period without sexual contact. Sometimes the shape of the vagina itself changes, becoming narrower, shorter, and less elastic, although it generally continues to be more than large enough for intercourse.

Pain and discomfort of any kind in the vaginal area should be taken seriously by women and by their physicians since pain obviously interferes with sexual pleasure and response. Several studies have found that the current generations of women of menopausal age and older do not tend to spontaneously report pain unless it is severe—so it is important that physicians ask directly if pain is present during sexual activity. In many cases physicians can tell during a vaginal exam whether a woman is likely to have pain due to vaginal atrophy, but this is not always the case. Other causes of pain are endometriosis, a fixed retroverted uterus, a prolapsed ovary, or water in the Fallopian tubes (hydrosalpinx)—all of which may need medical attention.

There is beginning evidence that women who have less vaginal atrophy have significantly higher blood levels of the male hormone androgen than do women with more vaginal atrophy—even though their blood estrogen levels are similar. Androgen, rather than estrogen, also appears to be the hormone most responsible for sexual desire and arousal in women as well as men. However, it is not known why some women (or men) have higher androgen levels. Nor is it currently medically advisable to administer androgen to women, because of potential masculinizing and other undesirable side effects.

With loss of estrogen, the usually acid vaginal secretions become less acidic, increasing the possibility of vaginal infection, and causing burning, itching, and discharge. This condition is variously called estrogen-deficient, steroid-deficient, atrophic, or "senile" vaginitis. If infection spreads to the bladder, it produces an inflammation called cystitis. These conditions are curable, but they should be treated by a doctor. Home douching should not be attempted unless your doctor instructs you to do so, because it can confuse the diagnosis and may not, in any case, be the recommended treatment. Douching may also aggravate vaginal dryness since it removes the normal secretions that coat the vaginal walls.

It should not be assumed that all vaginal itching and discharge reflect estrogen deficiency. There should be a complete examination, including the Pap test, to rule out the possibility of a tumor of the reproductive tract. Allergies, trichomoniasis, and yeast and fungus infections (especially in diabetics) are other causes of itching; womb prolapse (fallen womb) may produce a vaginal discharge.

With the thinning of the vaginal walls, the bladder and the urethra (the tube laying next to the vagina through which the urine is passed) are less protected and may be irritated during penile thrusting during intercourse. Women during or after menopause can develop what is sometimes called "honeymoon cystitis." This inflammation of the bladder, resulting from bruising and jostling, tends initially to be an irritative condition rather than a bacterial infection. When bacteria are present, however, it becomes full-fledged cystitis, characterized by an unrelenting, irresistible urge to urinate, accompanied by a burning sensation, and must be quickly treated medically. Advanced stages bring an increasingly painful burning (described as "exquisite" pain because of its unique character) during urination, waking at night to urinate, and, occasionally, blood in the urine.

The clitoris may be slightly reduced in size very late in life, although this is not always the case. The lips (or labia) of the vaginal opening may become thinner. The breasts may lose some of their support and become flatter and more pendulous. Pubic hair as well as scalp and underarm hair often becomes more sparse although facial hair may increase. The covering of the clitoris and the fat pad in the hair-covered public area lose some of their fatty tissue, leaving the clitoris less protected and thus more easily irritated. However, in spite of all these possible changes, the clitoris still remains the source of intense sexual sensation and orgasm, essentially as it was in earlier years.

Not all women show marked signs of estrogen loss after menopause. Some appear to produce enough estrogen in the adrenal glands to minimize the effects of estrogen loss in the ovaries. Obese women, particularly, show fewer effects after either hysterectomies or natural menopause. It is thought that this is because estrogen is converted in fat cells from hormones produced in the adrenal glands, principally androstenedione. Obese women thus have more estrogen available from this source.

Women in good health who were able to have orgasms in their younger years can often continue having orgasms until the end of their lives. (Indeed, some women begin to have orgasms for the first time as they grow older. Lack of orgasmic ability earlier in life does not necessarily mean that such a pattern will continue.) It is unclear whether the length of time required to reach orgasm changes with age in women. Nor do we know for certain whether there are changes in the duration and intensity of an orgasm with age. Shorter-lasting orgasms and spasms in the uterus, when they occur, may be evidence of hormonal imbalance.

Except for the effects of estrogen loss after menopause, the normal physical changes that accompany aging interfere little with female sexual ability. Some women become more relaxed about sex and may even enjoy it more, after menopause has freed them from fears of unwanted pregnancies. The frequency of sexual intercourse in women is much more affected by the age, health, and level of sexual functioning of their partner. Women may worry about orgasmic capacity, much as men are concerned about erection and ejaculatory capacity, but unlike most men, women can engage in sex even when they are emotionally upset or uninterested. They may not enjoy lovemaking or have an orgasm in such situations, but they are physically capable of having intercourse, especially with the aid of a lubricant. They are therefore spared the anxiety of nonperformance. Reports of decline of sexual interest in women as they age appear to be psychologically defensive or protective in origin rather than physiological. Women may be anticipating or actually experiencing a loss of sexual opportunity since the frequency of sexual intercourse in women is greatly affected by the age, health, and level of sexual interest and functioning of their partner.

MEN

NORMAL PHYSICAL CHANGES

Most men begin to worry about sexual aging sometime in their forties, when they compare their present level of sexual activity with their performance as teenagers and young adults. These worries tend to accelerate in the fifties and reach a peak in the sixties, as definite sexual changes continue to be observed.

What changes do men notice? Quite simply, their sex organs don't work in the same way as they did at a younger age. Lacking understanding of these changes, men may misinterpret them as alarming evidence of either the onset of impotence or its inevitability.

Potency is the man's capacity for sexual erection and ejaculation. Impotence, also called erectile dysfunction, is the temporary or permanent incapacity to have an erection sufficient to carry out the sexual act. (Sterility should not be confused with impotence. Sterility refers to infertility, or the incapacity to father children.) What is normal potency of one man may not be normal for another. There are variations in the frequency of erection, the length of time an erection is maintained, and the length of the time (the refractory period) before the next erection is possible. Such individual differences often continue over many years, indicating unique personal patterns. Therefore evaluations of a man's sexual status must be made in terms of his past and present history and not against some generalized standard involving comparisons with other men. Most sex therapists do not consider impotence or erectile dysfunction to be a problem unless it occurs in more than 25 percent of sexual encounters with the same partner.

Certain changes are far more likely than impotence per se. Allowing for great individual variations from man to man, a number of gradual and fairly predictable processes are associated with chronological aging. Somewhere in middle age, men ordinarily begin to take longer to obtain an erection than when they were younger: a few minutes after sexual stimulation rather than the few seconds required in adolescence. This is a critical piece of information for men to have, because it is precisely this slowly developing change that causes so many men to worry unnecessarily that they are entering the beginning stages of impotence. In midlife, many men find increased manual stimulation of the penis helpful in promoting arousal.

Somewhat later, perhaps in their late fifties or sixties, men may notice that their erections are not consistently quite as large, straight, and rigid as in previous years. Once the man is fully excited, however, his erection is likely to be sturdy and reliable, particularly if this was the pattern in earlier life. Manual stimulation by one's partner or oneself becomes even more important, along with other sensory and mental stimuli, such as the use of fantasy (see page 138).

The lubrication that appears prior to ejaculation (secreted by the Cowper's glands) is reduced or disappears completely as men age, but this has little effect on sexual performance. There are gradual changes in this secretory activity in the forties, which may not even be noticeable until the fifties or sixties. There is also a reduction in the volume of seminal fluid, and this results in a decrease in the need to ejaculate. Younger men produce three to five milliliters of semen (about one teaspoon) every twenty-four hours, while men past fifty produce two to three milliliters. This can be a decided advantage in lovemaking, since it means that the older man can usually delay ejaculation more easily and thus make love longer, extending his own enjoyment and enhancing the possibility of orgasm for his partner.

Orgasms may begin to feel different with age. The younger man is aware of a few pleasurable seconds just before ejaculation when he can no longer control himself. As ejaculation occurs, powerful contractions are felt and the semen spurts with a force that can carry it one to two feet from the tip of the penis. After gradual changes in midlife, a man of sixty or older may have a briefer period of awareness before ejaculation or no such period at all. (In some men, however, this anticipatory period lengthens because of spasm in the prostate.) The orgasm itself is generally less explosive, in that semen is propelled a shorter distance and contractions are not as forceful. The length of time required to reach orgasm may expand with aging. *None* of these physiological changes interferes with experiencing extreme orgasmic pleasure, even when pre-ejaculation awareness is altered or completely missing.

The forcefulness of orgasm also lessens naturally when a couple voluntarily prolong their lovemaking before orgasm. As they grow older, men have a choice of an extended period of sexual pleasure with a milder orgasm or a briefer session with a more intense orgasm.

Whereas younger men can usually have another ejaculation in a matter of minutes after orgasm, older men may need to wait a longer time (the refractory period), from a number of hours in midlife up to several days in late life, before an ejaculation is again possible. In addition, the older man may rapidly lose his erection following orgasm, sometimes so quickly that the penis literally slips out of the vagina. This is not a sign of impairment of the penis and its erectile capacity.

Men need not fall into the common trap of measuring manhood by the frequency with which they can carry intercourse through to ejaculation. Much of what is called "sexual decline" in later life has to do with a decline in ejaculatory frequency rather than a decline in sexual enjoyment. Many men approaching or past sixty are physically satisfied with one or two ejaculations per week (including ejaculation from masturbation), partly because less ejaculatory fluid has built up. Others, particularly if they were sexually less active earlier in life, do not ejaculate this frequently, although they can often force themselves to ejaculate more often. If left to choice, each man finds his own level. Remember that lovemaking need not, and in fact should not, be limited to ejaculatory ability. Men who are knowledgeable and comfortable about themselves may have intercourse with sturdy erections as frequently as they wish but ejaculate perhaps only once out of every two or three times that they make love. By delaying ejaculation, a man may be able to become erect over and over again, continuing with intercourse and the pleasurable feelings it arouses.

Comparing capacity for orgasm with that of women is also not useful, since women of all ages have in general a much greater capacity for frequent orgasms than men. This is one of the interesting differences between the sexes.

The testes may change in appearance with age, becoming smaller and less firm.

Male fertility—live and active sperm production—is generally thought to end in the mid-seventies, although new evidence is challenging this assumption. There are already documented cases of sperm production continuing into the nineties. A urologist can test for the presence of live sperm through microscopic examination of semen. The National Institute of Aging's ongoing studies of healthy men, beginning in 1958 and continuing up to the present, show that older men continue to ejaculate the same number of sperm as younger men, though the proportion of immature sperm seems to increase with age.

It is important to emphasize that fertility has no connection with potency (i.e. erectile capacity); even if a man loses his capacity to father children, his ability to have intercourse is not affected by loss of sperm production.

To summarize, physically healthy men do not lose their capacity to have erections and ejaculations as they age, although changes may occur. Differences in the sexual activity of healthy men as they grow older tend to reflect differences earlier in their lives in addition to changes with age. When problems appear, particularly impotence, they are caused by physical and/or psychological difficulties and are frequently improvable or even reversible.

IS THERE A MALE MENOPAUSE?

Testosterone appears to be the central hormone that influences sexual desire and performance in both men and women. Both sexes produce testosterone in small amounts in the adrenal glands. In addition, males produce large amounts in their testes. Do men experience a period in life that is physically or psychologically comparable to the female cessation of menstruation and loss of estrogen hormones? There is certainly no physical "menopause" or climacteric in men analogous to that in women, because hormone loss in men, when it occurs at all, does not occur precipitously. (Actually, estrogen loss in women during menopause occurs in spurts, and never in a single, abrupt cessation.) Decreases in the production of testosterone in the testes take place very gradually, if at all, as men grow older, and there are wide individual variations. Early studies of testosterone, which showed some decline with aging, included obese, alcoholic, and/or chronically ill subjects. It is speculated that poor health rather than aging may have been the culprit here. A component of the National Institute on Aging study, involving seventy-six healthy, vigorous men aged twenty-five to eighty-nine, found that testosterone levels remained remarkably stable after age thirty. Some men in very late age have testosterone levels identical with those in young men.

Few men have specific physiological symptoms that can be traced directly to lowered testosterone levels. Even castrated men, whose testes have been removed, may be able to have erections for years. It appears that the relative proportions of testosterone and estradiol (the most potent naturally occurring estrogen in humans) may be important in determining male sexual function. A testosterone level below 300 nanograms percent (one nanogram equals one millionth of a gram for each tenth of a liter of blood) in males (and 10 nanograms percent in females) is considered a potential cause of sexual problems, but this level is rare.

Distinct psychological symptoms related to testosterone changes, such as depression, are also rare and can usually be accounted for by other circumstances in a man's life, such as his reactions to middle age, to retirement, to aging in general, or to other losses and stresses.

As research on male hormone levels becomes more sophisticated and reliable, a male climacteric may eventually be identifiable, particularly with reference to some of the sexual changes that now accompany male aging. However, it will be quite different from our concept of female menopause, with far less distinct and less predictable symptoms.

PHYSICAL SEXUAL CHANGES—SIGNS OF AGING OR DISEASE?

We do not yet know whether all the physiological changes we have described in this chapter are "normal aging" processes or symptoms of reversible physical conditions. The fact that a man takes longer to achieve an erection as he gets older, or requires a longer period of time before an erection can occur again after the last sexual act, may possibly be related to reduced nutritive, oxygen, and blood supplies because of hardening of the arteries (arteriosclerosis). From a variety of recent studies we already know that much physical change that has been attributed to aging is in fact due to a variety of other factors, notably the vascular diseases. The integrative systems of the body, which link so many of its functions—the circulatory system, the endocrine or hormonal system, the central nervous system, all play a role in the decline of functioning when they are affected by disease. We are only beginning to have some knowledge of the fundamentals of the aging process itself: for example, whether there is a central nervous system "pacemaker" that dictates change, or whether there are reductions in the speed of reactions and in metabolism.

Interest in sex or sexual desire is believed to decline only slightly with age in healthy men, according to current studies. In fact, desire does not necessarily change even in those men who experience a loss of erectile capacity or a change in orgasmic frequency. But the amount of sexual activity itself, beyond normal ejaculatory declines, does tend to decrease. Some speculate that this may be influenced by changes in the central nervous system that reduce the male's ability to translate visual sexual stimuli into physical arousal. Other factors may be disease processes under way but not yet obvious.

Finally, the factor of the unavailability or undesirability of one's mate obviously influences sexual activity.

It is possible that in the future we will find sexual activity actually improving with age as we increasingly separate the diseases of later life, as well as psychological impairments, from aging processes, and begin to prevent and treat these diseases and impairments on a wide scale. Furthermore, if aging factors become more clear-cut and if agents that will directly retard the process of aging are found, there will be still further changes in the sexual picture. For example, estrogen replacement therapy for women clearly reduces or reverses the effects of menopausal estrogen loss. However, many questions remain about its safe use (see Chapter 6). What relatively healthy men and women need to remember, even under the limitations of our present knowledge about aging, is that sexual activity—to whatever degree and in whatever forms they want to express it—should continue to be possible, normal, pleasurable, and beneficial. Individuals with fairly common chronic ailments can also adapt their sexual desires to satisfactory expression in many cases. Neither aging nor most infirmity need automatically spell the end of sex.

3

THE EFFECTS OF COMMON
MEDICAL PROBLEMS ON SEX

By their forties and fifties, many people became more aware of physical changes in their bodies—a little osteoarthritis in the knee, some high blood pressure, a touch of raised cholesterol, faster heartbeat when climbing stairs. At the same time, heart disease and other disorders become serious concerns. Over 70 percent of persons over age forty-five have one or more chronic physical conditions. (One in ten persons in the adult population has a disability that produces a definitive handicap of one kind or another.) This is the time when people typically begin to take their bodies more seriously. A growing number of individuals adopt new health practices or revitalize old ones, with good evidence that they can help slow the aging process and even avoid a number of the disorders associated with it.

But what happens when illness strikes? Obviously illness, acute and chronic, affects people sexually. An acute illness, which is sudden and severe, has an immediate effect. The body becomes totally involved in meeting the physical threat, and anxiety is strong until the crisis has passed and the full extent of the illness is known. Understandably, people in these circumstances seldom have interest in sexuality. Once the acute phase is over, most people return slowly to sexuality; but if recovery time is lengthy or if the illness is chronic or disabling there can be accompanying sexual problems. Here we discuss several of the more common conditions that may directly affect sexuality in persons over forty.

HEART DISEASE

In the forty-five–sixty-four age group, the occurrence of heart disease is nearly three times as great in men as in women. After sixty-five the rates become more equalized, and it is believed that postmenopausal women are less protected than before, because of reduction in estrogen levels.

Heart (coronary) attacks lead many people to give up sex altogether under the assumption that it will endanger their lives. Recent studies show that 60–75 percent of couples decrease or stop sexual activity after a heart attack, many because their doctors fail to give them adequate advice about sex. Studies also show that the person who does resume sexual activity usually waits about sixteen weeks. Those with the most active sex life before a coronary attack resume sex soonest. Many experts believe that an eight-to-fourteen-week waiting period is adequate before resumption of sexual intercourse, depending on the patient's interest, general fitness, and conditioning. Self-stimulation or mutual masturbation may be an alternative and usually can be started earlier than sexual intercourse. Some propose a functional test to determine when it is safe to resume: If you can walk briskly (two to two and a half miles per hour) for three blocks without distress in the chest, pain, palpitations, or shortness of breath, you are usually well enough for sexual exertion.

Sex can be carried out safely after a heart attack without sacrificing pleasure and quality. Studies show that on the average, couples take ten to sixteen minutes for the more physically rigorous part of the sex act. The oxygen usage (or "cost") in sex approximates climbing one or two flights of stairs, walking rapidly at a rate of two to two and a half miles per hour, or completing many common occupational tasks. In average sexual activity the heart rate ranges from 90 to 170 beats per minute, which is the level for light to moderate physical activity. The maximum increase occurs with orgasm, when the average heart rate is 120 beats per minute for about fifteen or twenty seconds. Systolic blood pressure (the upper reading, which reflects the contraction phase of the heart's action) may double from 120 to over 240 (with an average of 162), and the respiratory rate rises from sixteen–eighteen to about sixty breaths per minute. These vital signs increase only slightly more in men than in women when the man takes the position on top during sex. Intercourse conducted side by side or with the woman on top is recommended to reduce the exertion of the man if he is the one with the heart problem. These positions avoid sapping of energy from prolonged use of the arms and legs to support the body. Proper physical conditioning (usually a program of brisk walking and/or swimming) under the doctor's guidance can also be useful, in part because the pulse-rate rise during sex can be lowered by conditioning.

Physical fitness programs enhance heart performance for a variety of activities, including sex. A useful book for exercise ideas after a heart attack is *The Cardiologists' Guide to Fitness and Health Through Exercise* by L. R. Zohman and A. A. Kattus (Simon & Schuster, 1979). Isometric exercises may be unwise for certain kinds of patients because they cause pressure changes in the aorta, the major blood vessel from the heart. Check with your physician.

Before undertaking an exercise program you can ask your doctor to arrange a "stress EKG," special testing in which an electrocardiogram or EKG (an instrument that traces the heart's electric currents and provides information regarding the heart's actions in health and disease) is taken while you are conducted through various levels of exercise. An electromagnetic tape recording of a person's EKG during the sexual act can be made, in the privacy of his or her own home, although such a test is not routine, or easily available. This Sexercise Tolerance Test was developed by Drs. Hellerstein and Friedman, who, through monitors in their patients' homes, studied the sexual activity of men after recovery from acute heart attacks. They concluded that if the patient could perform exercise at levels of vigorous walking and other special activities without symptoms of abnormal pulse rate, blood pressure, or EKG changes, it was generally safe to recommend the resumption of sexual activity.

Some physicians warn that stress tests are not infallible. They can produce false alarms for healthy people, while coronary disease may not be registered. A medical and sexual history, the patient's report on chest pain during exertion, as well as an electrocardiogram taken during rest should all be part of the stress examination.

It must be remembered that physical exercise itself lessens likelihood of a heart attack. The sedentary person seems to be more prone to coronary attacks and less apt to survive if one occurs. Too much food and drink before sexual activity can also place a strain on the heart. Of course, if the condition of the heart has deteriorated to the point that attack is imminent, it will occur with any physical exertion, not merely sex. Many everyday nonsexual activities that people are not likely to give up produce more increased heart and respiratory rates than sexual intercourse.

It should also be realized that sexual arousal alone affects the vital signs—although not as intensely as the later stages of sexual activity. Thus failure to provide sexual release may prolong arousal, causing psychological frustration that may produce adverse physical effects.

Potency problems can follow a heart attack for both physical and psychological reasons. Chest pain (angina pectoris) a man may experience as the result of various forms of exertion is distracting during sex and discourages erection. To counteract this pain, coronary dilators such as nitroglycerin, prescribed by a physician, can be taken just prior to intercourse to improve circulation and reduce pain. A second common and understandable cause of potency problems is fear of inducing another coronary and risking death. The patient's partner, fearing the occurrence of another coronary attack, also may lose sexual desire and avoid sexual activity. Yet the incidence of death during intercourse is estimated at less than 1 percent of sudden coronary deaths. (In a major Japanese study, the rate was less than 0.6 percent. Of this small percentage, a majority of deaths occurred in extramarital relations, suggesting that the stressful aspects associated with such affairs, such as hurry, guilt, and anxiety, are a factor.)

Depression and anxiety are common up to a year after a heart attack. Irritability, exhaustion, and feelings of loss may be present. Patients may believe their wife or husband is no longer attracted to them. Spouses may become overly protective and fearful of upsetting the patient. It should be made clear that all these normal reactions to what has been a frightening experience will in most cases subside with time. Talking about such feelings with the physician or with a psychotherapist can offer relief and may help to avoid problems with the relationship and, more specifically, with sex.

After the resumption of sexual activity, the patient should report the following to his or her doctor: (1) anginal pain occurring during or after sex; (2) palpitation continuing fifteen minutes or more afterward; (3) unusual episodes of sleeplessness after sexual exertion; (4) marked fatigue the next day. Stress can be lessened by: (1) having sex with a familiar and considerate partner; (2) waiting three hours or more after eating or drinking alcohol; (3) using a room with a moderate temperature; (4) choosing a time when the patient is relaxed, such as the morning after a restful night. If the patient begins to feel strained or anxious during sexual activity, he or she should simply stop and breathe deeply for a few minutes before beginning again.

Physicians do not always advise their patients adequately on the resumption of sexual relations after a heart attack. They may be too conservative or fail to realize the importance of sex to the patient. If you want to know more than your doctor has told you, it may be necessary to ask for specific information and directions, including a program of physical conditioning. The best time to ask is when you are still in the hospital or immediately afterward. Your sexual partner also needs to be fully informed of your condition and counseled about any changes in life-style, including lovemaking, that may be necessary. Under most circumstances there is little reason to abstain from sex after a heart attack, and many reasons to continue. Pleasure, exhilaration, release of tension, mild exercise, and a sense of well-being are some of the benefits. Many couples report a new enjoyment of intimacy, and of each other, as a result of the appreciation of life that a brush with mortality can bring.

Episodes of congestive heart failure are also commonly called heart attacks. When this condition is effectively managed by digitalis, diuretics, and diet, sexual activity can be part of the final recovery process. Two or three weeks for recovery is advised before resuming sex. As a test for readiness, you should be able to walk briskly for three blocks without shortness of breath.

Patients with cardiac pacemakers need not give up sex. Limitations on all forms of physical activity are advised during the first two weeks following implantation, to allow healing. Otherwise the guideline to follow is an evaluation of the underlying cardiac condition.

CORONARY BYPASS SURGERY

Coronary bypass surgery is now such a frequently performed surgical procedure that we wish to deal separately with its sexual ramifications. Because of symptoms, treatment of the disease, or fear of sudden death from sexual activity, many patients have sexual dysfunctions by the time they are candidates for the surgery. Coronary bypass surgery may not always prolong life, but it does often improve the quality of a life, by relieving pain and other symptoms. Further, it may relieve or even eliminate sexual dysfunction.

Patients and their partners need to learn specifically how healing occurs after surgery so they can gauge its progress. Physicians should inform them, for example, that the chest bones require three months to heal totally and become stable. Patients must know what level of activity they can undertake during this time without danger of stressing the chest bones and causing separation. It is also common to misinterpret pain caused by the chest wall wound as angina. The chest wall pain will disappear with time. Leg wounds caused by removing veins for replacement in the chest heal in about two weeks, but may be uncomfortable longer, and physical activity may aggravate this condition in the early stages of healing.

Most patients are urged to walk and otherwise move about very soon after the surgery. Exercise programs undertaken to improve heart capacity can be very reassuring to patients who fear resuming sexual activity. One technique is to begin walking daily, until gradually the patient can walk steadily for half an hour, gradually increasing to three miles a day. Finally, patients are asked to work, again gradually, toward walking three miles a day in forty-five minutes or less. When this goal is reached, it is usually physically safe to resume sexual activity. If patients remain anxious, they can be reassured by a treadmill test that demonstrates that their heart is not overstressed by a high level of activity.

Because of their previous experience with chest pain, it is common for patients to become psychologically dependent on nitroglycerin before sexual activity, even though surgery may have eliminated the need for it. Encouragement from other patients who have weaned themselves from nitroglycerin can be very helpful. If this does not work, a mild antianxiety medication used for a brief time may assist the patient over this hurdle.

Some patients have complications that may call for special counseling. Those who require medications such as beta blockers, which can decrease sexual desire and cause impotence, may be able to switch to other medications, such as calcium blockers like verapamil, with fewer sexual side effects. Those with arrhythmias (irregular heartbeat) that do not require treatment need reassurance and perhaps a heart monitor (the Holter monitor) or a treadmill test to calm anxiety about sexual activity. When antiarrhythmic drugs and beta blockers cannot be avoided, patients need to understand that such drugs are life-protective, and should be encouraged to explore other forms of intimacy and physical pleasure.

Most coronary bypass surgery patients, including those with more than one bypass surgery, experience relief of heart symptoms and, frequently, a return to a reasonable level of sexual activity. The chances for this are improved with a careful exercise and conditioning program. Brief treatment of anxiety and depression with drugs that are acceptable for heart patients can be extremely helpful toward resumption of sexual functioning. Such drugs can often be discontinued in a few weeks as the patient gains his or her own momentum. Long-range use of antidepressant drugs is seldom helpful for a depressed coronary patient. Counseling, psychotherapy, and provision of information about heart attacks is much more successful.

HYPERTENSION

It is safe for most patients with hypertension—high blood pressure—to have sex. Since many people with hypertension have no significant impairment of heart function, men or women with average to moderate hypertension need not restrict themselves sexually. They should, however, have their hypertension well controlled by diet, physical exercise, and, when appropriate, drug therapy. Very severe cases of hypertension may require some modification of sexual activity; your doctor is the best judge of this.

Men with untreated hypertension are reported to have about a 15 percent incidence of impotence. The effects of hypertension on female sexuality have not been as well studied. Sexual impairment can be avoided by proper treatment of hypertension. Weight loss if one is overweight, regular exercise, reduction of cholesterol levels, limitation of salt to five grams or less a day, moderate use of alcohol, and no smoking are the first steps in treatment. If these do not bring blood pressure down to acceptable levels, medication is necessary. Such medication must be carefully chosen to avoid side effects of impaired sexual response (see Chapter 8).

STROKE

The average age at which stroke (cerebrovascular accident) occurs is about seventy years. Long-standing untreated hypertension is a major cause of stroke. Strokes do not necessitate the permanent discontinuance of sexual activity, but it is very common to experience problems in many areas, including sexuality, immediately after a stroke. Unless a stroke causes severe trauma to the brain, sexual desire often remains undamaged; performance is more likely to be affected. Recovery depends on the patient's general health before the stroke, the severity of the stroke, and the patient's motivation, among other factors. Many patients have preexisting health problems such as diabetes or coronary artery disease, and these disorders as well as medications taken to control them may contribute to sexual problems.

Depression is almost universal among patients in the early months after a stroke. Depression often lifts as patients adapt and see signs of their own recovery, including a return to sexual functioning at whatever level is feasible. Intimacy through touching and communication of feelings, whether sexual or not, can become an important part of recovery.

Some degree of weakness on one side of the body is common after stroke, although improvement is often possible. If paralysis or a significant loss of use occurs on the affected side, along with a decrease in sensation, couples who make a succesful adjustment learn to compensate by emphasizing the noninvolved side in lovemaking. Steadying oneself by a hand on the headboard, bracing a foot against the footboard, or using pillows as supports can help. Persons who have had a stroke usually function best sexually on their back. A useful reference for stroke patients and their mates is D. C. Renshaw's article "Sexual Problems in Stroke Patients" in the journal *Medical Aspects of Human Sexuality*, December 1975 (available in medical libraries).

It is important to know that sexual activity has not been found to be a factor in bringing on a stroke or in causing more damage to persons who have had a stroke. The partner of a female stroke patient may develop temporary impotence because of the fear of damage to her, and he needs reassurance. Among male stroke patients, some experience potency problems and others do not. Careful evaluation helps reveal when problems are treatable and reversible.

DIABETES

One in every twenty persons in the United States now has sugar diabetes (diabetes mellitus). One form of it, type I diabetes, thought to be possibly viral in origin, typically develops in persons under age twenty-five, who then become dependent on insulin for the rest of their lives and cannot survive without it. Type II diabetes occurs mainly after age forty. Ninety percent of person afflicted with Type II are overweight or obese, and many have atherosclerosis. A family history of diabetes is common. Management often focuses first on weight loss, exercise, and careful diet rather than insulin. Diabetes is a special problem in later life since 40 percent of known diabetics are aged sixty-five or older. (A proportion of older persons are misdiagnosed as diabetic or prediabetic because they don't react as well to glucose tolerance tests as do younger people. Their reaction may simply be a feature of aging rather than a sign of diabetes.)

Most men with diabetes are not impotent, but it is one of the few illnesses that can directly cause chronic impotence in men. Impotence occurs two to five times as often in diabetic men as in the general population, even though sexual interest and desire often continue unabated. Indeed, the gradual, persistent occurrence of impotence is often the first symptom of diabetes. Many cases of diabetic-produced impotence are reversible. If the disease has been unrecognized or poorly controlled, there is a fair chance that diagnosis and proper regulation thereafter will improve potency. Many patients learn to monitor their blood glucose level, aided by a proper diet, exercise, and medications such as oral hypoglycemic agents or a regimen of insulin. When impotence occurs in already well-controlled diabetes, it may be permanent. (One factor involved may be that such diabetes is caused by a change in the cell receptor ability to use insulin rather than a lack of insulin per se.) In addition, in those who have been diabetic for a long time, the chances are greater that the impotence will be chronic and irreversible. However, physicians should always look for other conditions that may be causing impotence. A common cause is a thyroid condition that may accompany diabetes. Thyroid replacement therapy may bring dramatic results.

Current research strongly suggests that sexuality is affected far less by diabetes in women than in men. Max Ellenberg, diabetes specialist at the Mount Sinai Medical Center in New York, found little change in orgasmic response due to the presence or absence of neuropathy (disturbance in the peripheral nervous system) and other complications among female diabetics. Furthermore, female diabetics did not differ appreciably from the general female population in orgasm frequency. Ellenberg was unable to find any anatomical, neurological, or physiological explanation for women diabetics' faring better sexually than men. One possible explanation is that they have a psychological advantage that is as yet not understood. Ellenberg had to rely solely on women's own statements since he had no objective measures of female sexual response, but assuming that the women in his study were both accurate in their statements and representative of female diabetics in general, the conclusion is that sexual functioning in diabetic women appears to remain unchanged from previous functioning.

CHRONIC PROSTATITIS

Inflammation or infection of the genitals or the urinary tract is the most common cause of temporary sexual dysfunction in males. Males in their twenties and thirties may have bouts of such inflammation, causing burning and painful urination, fever, or discharge. Treatment with antibiotics is usually effective.

If the prostate becomes infected, a specific inflammation called prostatitis may become chronic or recurrent, and be accompanied by diminished sexual desire due predominantly to pain or discomfort. The prostate gland is a walnut-sized organ located just beneath the bladder. It produces the milky lubricating fluid that transports sperm during sexual intercourse. Prostatitis is characterized by a history of cloudy white discharge from the penis which usually appears in the morning or while straining on the toilet. Pain may occur in the perineal region (the area between the scrotum and the anus) and in the end of the penis on urination and ejaculation. Upon massage, the prostate feels tender.

Treatment includes antibiotics, warm sitz baths, and periodic gentle prostatic massage by a physician to milk excess fluid from the gland. There is no convincing evidence that zinc taken orally helps chronic prostatitis. Some believe that the practice of Kegel exercises, originally designed for females, may help (see pages 113–14). Improvement after treatment may take several weeks or as long as six months, since chronic prostatitis can be difficult to eradicate completely and may recur over time. Sexual desire usually returns after pain lessens, especially when the pain after ejaculation is eliminated. With chronic prostatitis, one should avoid an excess of alcohol, coffee, or spicy foods (which make one thirsty) since excessive fluid intake may lead to retention of urine following sexual intercourse.

It has recently been discovered that up to half or more prostate infections are caused by the major U.S. venereal disease, chlamydia, and are transmitted by sexual contact. Once diagnosed, this bacterium responds to antibiotics.

Mild prostatitis may be the basis for some pain between the anus and the scrotum after ejaculation. Congestive prostatitis, another form of the affliction, can be caused by too frequent as well as too infrequent sex. Congestion may be induced by excessive preliminary sexual arousal, or an unsatisfying orgasm. More commonly, infrequent sex results in congestion in the pelvic area. Treatment consists of more frequent sexual release as well as prostatic massage and warm sitz baths.

ARTHRITIS

Arthritis is a widespread condition that affects forty million Americans, and strikes women twice as often as men. Rheumatoid arthritis, commonly beginning between ages twenty-five and fifty, and osteoarthritis, a later-life condition, are the two major forms of arthritis and may cause pain during sexual activity. Medications such as simple aspirin are used to reduce pain. It is reassuring to know that most drugs used to treat arthritis, except for corticosteroids, do not interfere with either sexual desire or sexual performance. Experimentation with new sexual positions that do not aggravate pain in sensitive joints is often helpful. A well-established program of exercise, rest, and warm baths is especially useful in reducing arthritic discomfort and in facilitating sex. Indeed, much of the crippling by rheumatoid arthritis results from inactivity. A person tends to keep painful joints in comfortable positions, and they become stiffened, even "frozen." For information on exercise and other treatments, write for the free publication list published by the Arthritis Foundation, 115 East 18th Street, New York, N.Y. 10003. Several reprints on sexuality and arthritis are also available.

Hip discomfort is perhaps the most frequent arthritic problem that affects sexual activity. Hip action during sex may be slowed down or made difficult because of pain or changes in the ability to move the hips. When the problem is severe, surgical hip replacement may restore function, including that involved in sex. For less severe conditions, a range of therapies can be beneficial. Exercise, prescribed by your doctor, should include a full range of motion for the joints, strengthening and stretching of muscles, and engaging in the usual household and outside activities. It is also important to maintain an erect position when standing and walking, sit upright in a straight-back chair, and rest in bed for short periods several times during the day. In general, those with this problem should rest or sleep in a straight position, flat on the back, using a small pillow under the head (a pillow under the knees can lead to stiff, bent knees).

Heat relaxes muscle spasm and is useful before undertaking an exercise program and also prior to sex. Various types of heat can be used, such as heat lamps, heating pads, warm compresses, tub baths, showers, and paraffin baths. A daily tub bath with warm—but not hot—water and for no more than twenty minutes is excellent. (Longer than that can be fatiguing.) The use of a water bed and massage oils may enhance comfort. During sexual activity the side-by-side position—either face to face or back to front—may be preferred by both men and women, especially when the patient has many tender areas and pain trigger points. Experiment until you find positions that work best for you. Pillows can help cushion painful joints.

Timing can also be important. Some discover that pain and stiffness diminish or disappear completely at certain times of day; sexual activity can be planned for these times. Those with rheumatoid arthritis often feel greater pain and stiffness in the morning, while for those with osteoarthritis, morning is usually the best time of day, with discomfort increasing at the end of the day. Ask your doctor to time pain or anti-inflammatory medications so they will be most effective at times when you are most likely to have sexual activity. A condition known as Sjögren's syndrome occurs with some forms of arthritis and results in a decrease in body secretions. A lubricant like K-Y jelly will compensate for inadequate vaginal secretions.

There is evidence that regular sex activity may produce some relief from the pain of rheumatoid arthritis for four to eight hours, probably because of adrenal gland production of the hormone cortisone, and because of the physical activity involved. The body's release of endorphins, its natural pain relievers, during sexual activity and especially during orgasm may also be a factor. Finally, emotional stress can result from sexual dissatisfaction, and since stress worsens arthritis, satisfying sexual activity can be helpful in maintaining good functioning.

BACKACHE

Aches in the small of the back near the base of the spine are common in mid and later life. Perhaps the most frequent cause is strain produced by sudden use of back muscles in a generally inactive person. In older women it can be caused by osteoporosis (post-menopausal softening of the bones), related to reduction of estrogen levels. Slipped disks, arthritis, and simply poor posture are other causes of backache in both men and women.

A firm mattress is needed by most backache sufferers, as well as a bed board—a plywood board at least one-half inch thick and the same size as the mattress, placed between mattress and springs for extra support. Exercise is helpful for most forms of backache, but see your doctor for individualized instructions. Slipped disks—disks are rubbery white oval shock absorbers located between pairs of vertebra in the spine—often respond well to exercise but sometimes require prolonged bed rest; otherwise surgery may be necessary. Since the 1960s, chymopapain, an experimental drug extracted from papaya, has been used to treat back ailments as an alternative to surgery. In 1982 it was approved for general use by the FDA. An enzyme similar to a meat tenderizer, the drug is injected directly into the disk, which it dissolves. This procedure, which relieves pain and pressure on nerves, is most useful in patients aged thirty to fifty. Results are not uniformly positive and may include certain complications.

Sufferers from arthritic backache should follow the program described above for arthritis. Sexual activity itself is an excellent form of exercise therapy for the back, stomach, and pelvic muscles, and if undertaken in a regular and reasonably vigorous manner it can help reduce back pain. During sex, the side position may be most comfortable if back muscles are tender. Or the backache sufferer may prefer to lie on his or her back, with the partner on top. Areas of discomfort can be supported by pillows.

ANEMIA

One out of four people over sixty and somewhat fewer people in midlife have some measure of anemia, a common cause of fatigue and consequent reduction of sexual activity. Anemia may develop insidiously following even a mild general or localized infection, or as the result of a poor diet. It is also frequently seen in women who menstruate heavily around menopause. Tiredness, loss of appetite, and headaches are some of its early manifestations. Since anemia is the symptom of a number of diseases, comprehensive medical examination is indicated. Follow-up treatment is important. Often an improved diet with adequate vitamins and minerals is all that is necessary to restore energy—and sexual activity.

CHRONIC CYSTITIS AND URETHRITIS

Some women experience recurrent outbreaks of cystitis and urethritis following intercourse. The cause is often unclear. The chief symptoms are severe pain and burning around the urethra. If no organisms can be found in their urine, such women are often told their problem is psychological. This leads to outrage at the doctor and to depression, continued pain, and a sense of hopelessness.

Do not give up. The diagnostic process may have to be ongoing until the cause or causes are found and corrected. The merits of surgical correction, medications, education on sexual techniques and positions, pain management, and interpersonal counseling should all be weighed. A woman's sexual partner should be checked for possible untreated prostatitis. The depression that usually accompanies chronic cystitis needs to be dealt with. Above all, the physician should persist, and the woman should not be told it is all in her head. Even long-standing cystitis can be evaluated and cured.

STRESS INCONTINENCE

Stress incontinence, a common problem for women, is caused by stretched pelvic muscles that allow the uterus to extend down into the vaginal cavity, putting pressure on the bladder. This can lead to a seepage of urine because of momentary inability to control the bladder, particularly when a woman laughs, coughs, engages in sex, or otherwise exerts herself. Dyspareunia, or painful intercourse, may accompany the condition. Stress incontinence is very common, but it is seen most frequently in women with a number of children, who may have had unrepaired injuries following childbirth, with resulting relaxation of the supports of the uterus and bladder. Menopause, with its loss of estrogen, may also contribute to slack pelvic organs. Stress incontinence may be seen in women who have had their uterus removed surgically (hysterectomy). Weak supporting tissues cause the bladder to protrude into the vagina (cystocele).

Temporary relief of this form of mild incontinence can sometimes be obtained through inserting a large tampon in the vagina, which gives support to the bladder. This technique can be helpful in situations when a woman may not have easy access to a toilet. However, the tampon should not be left in place for more than a few hours because of the danger of toxic shock syndrome from extended use of a tampon.

Estrogen taken by mouth or applied locally in the form of cream may reduce urethral stiffness and help firm up the vaginal lining, thus reducing the irritation from the protruding bladder (see Chapter 6). A number of other drugs are available to reduce bladder contractions or improve muscle tone, but few have been tested on women of menopausal age or older, and all have possible side effects, which range from constipation and mucous membrane dryness to dizziness, drowsiness, and confusion.

Urinating every two hours or less is a simpler and often effective solution. Many women wear a thin disposable pad to protect their clothing in case of leakage. Kegel exercises (see pages 113–14) are very useful, whether the problem is a "dropped uterus" or a "dropped bladder." Biofeedback training may bring improvement. In severe cases, surgery may be required to reposition the internal pelvic organs and tighten muscles. Such surgery can be done under local or spinal anesthesia in less than an hour. The hospital stay can be as short as three days and the surgical success rate is very high. A self-help and advocacy organization called HIP (Help for Incontinent People) can provide information and lists of resources. Write to HIP, Department RBC, P.O. Box 544, Union, S.C. 29379, and include a business-sized self-addressed and stamped envelope.

Herniation of the rectum (rectocele) may occur alone or in association with prolapse of the bladder. Surgical treatment is usually effective for rectoceles.

PARKINSON'S DISEASE

Parkinson's disease is a progressive nervous-system disorder of the middle and later years, marked by tremor, slowness of movement, partial facial paralysis, and peculiarity of posture and gait. Depres-

the disease and in a few cases, when the penis is angled too far, sex becomes impossible. However, in about 90 percent of cases of Peyronie's disease, sex can continue, even though there may be some pain. This ailment is thought to be rare, but our own experience in talking with physicians and patients leads us to suspect that it may be more common than is believed. Psychotherapy can be helpful, enabling men to adjust to changes in the physical appearance of the penis as well as changes in functioning.

CHRONIC RENAL DISEASE

Patients with chronic renal disease experience a continuum of treatments which may end with renal dialysis or renal transplants. This can be a stressful disease, often associated with depression and/or anxiety. Male chronic renal patients are often sterile and may have reduced levels of serum testosterone. Other organic factors affecting sexuality may be present, although they have not been identified. Nonetheless, not all renal patients have sexual problems and those who do may be treatable if the problems are not strictly organic. Treatment of anxiety and depression and the use of marital counseling can be effective. Kidney transplants often restore sexual capacity.

CHRONIC EMPHYSEMA AND BRONCHITIS

Chronic emphysema and bronchitis, which entail shortness of breath, often hinder physical activity, including sex. The extent of the limitation depends on the severity of the disease. Resting at intervals, and finding the least physically taxing ways to have sex, help. When shortness of breath is severe, oxygen can be used during sexual activity; a long tube attached to an oxygen tank and fixed to the patient's nostrils allows freedom of movement.

HERNIA OR RUPTURE

A hernia or rupture is the protrusion of a part of the intestine through a gap or weak point in the muscular abdominal wall that contains it. The main complication to avoid is strangulation—the cutting off of the blood supply, with resulting death of tissue—which is a true surgical emergency. Fear of aggravating a hernia with sexual activity is common and may be justified. Straining of any kind, including straining during sexual intercourse, can increase hernia symptoms such as pain and, rarely, induce strangulation. Many surgeons recommend corrective surgery early rather than waiting for an emergency to arise.

If sex has been discontinued for a medical reason for any length of time, some readjustment will be necessary once it is resumed. Irregular or infrequent sexual stimulation can interfere with healthy sexual functioning, adversely affecting potency in men and lubrication, vaginal shape, and muscle tone in women. These difficulties are likely to taper off as activity is resumed, and one should not be discouraged by initial problems. If former sexual activities are no longer viable for medical reasons, new ones can be explored. When a sexual partner is not available (as, for example, in widowhood) or circumstances do not permit contact with a partner, both men and women can protect much of their sexual capacity through regular self-stimulation (masturbation) if this is comfortable for them.

Continued sexuality in the face of illness or disability requires confronting anxieties, getting facts, finding out what adjustments have to be made, and reaching the best solutions possible. Intimacy does not have to be sacrificed in all this and may in fact increase as couples search together for ways to handle the effects of medical problems on sexuality.

In summary, the most common fears surrounding illness, disability, and sexuality are that sex may cause pain, injury, or in certain cases, even death. Many fear that the physical changes resulting from illness or disability will lead to sexual unattractiveness and undesirability.

To combat difficulties and fears:

- Talk to your doctor as often as you need to. Get the best medical advice on how to proceed with sexual activity as safely and comfortably as possible.
- Talk to your partner about the issues that concern both of you—not just once but on an ongoing basis.

- Talk to other people who have the same physical problems, especially if they seem to have made good adjustments. Join support groups when they are available for specific illnesses and physical conditions.
- Consider psychotherapy if problems persist.

4

SEXUALLY TRANSMITTED DISEASES

One in four Americans between ages fifteen and fifty-five will acquire a sexually transmitted disease (STD) at some point in his or her life. Less is known about the incidence among those who are over fifty-five. STDs are the world's most common communicable diseases. Incidence has increased steadily in the United States over the past fifteen years, due to a greater number and variety of sexual practices, to a population that moves about readily, and to the emergence of strains of sexually transmitted organisms that are resistant to antibodies. As a result, we find ourselves in a peculiar position, with growing acceptance of many sexual practices countered by a growing worry about the possibility of acquiring a sexually transmittable disease, especially currently incurable ones like genital herpes or AIDS. A recent Gallup poll found more people than ever before, of all ages, accepting of premarital sex and equal sexual freedom for men and women, but other polls suggest that the country is entering a new phase of anxiety about sexuality, partly as a reaction against the permissiveness of the 1960s and 1970s but more importantly because of fears of difficult-to-treat and fatal sexually transmitted diseases. According to a nationwide NBC News/Wall Street Journal poll released in January 1986, 18 percent of people who are single, divorced, or separated have changed their sexual behavior because of fear of AIDS. Three percent of married people have done so as well. Half of those who changed said they were using condoms more frequently and over 90 percent were more careful about choosing partners and avoiding casual sex or promiscuity.

Twenty-five or so diseases are known to spread through sexual contact. Except for AIDS, which thus far has primarily affected the male homosexual community, STDs affect women and newborns most severely, although men suffer much discomfort as well.

ACQUIRED IMMUNE DEFICIENCY SYNDROME (AIDS)

AIDS, a disease that destroys the body's immune system and leads inevitably to death, usually from infection, was first recognized in the U.S. in 1977–78. The current best guess about its origins is that it began in central Africa in the early 1970s as a result of transmission from infected animals to humans. It has become the focus of intense concern on the part of the health profession and the general public. AIDS is caused by a blood-borne virus known as HTLV-III and is transmitted by the exchange of certain body fluids, especially through sexual contact that opens a blood channel in either mucous membranes or broken skin, and through intravenous (IV) drug use. Casual, nonsexual contact is not thought to transmit AIDS. Although low concentrations of the AIDS virus have been found in tears, urine, saliva, and in a few cases vaginal fluid, there have been no documented cases of AIDS transmission by these routes. Housemates, family members, and medical personnel caring for AIDS patients have not become infected while providing care. Hugging and ordinary kissing of AIDS patients is not dangerous and is, in fact, encouraged as part of maintaining their emotional health. The primary and perhaps sole agents of transmission are AIDS-infected blood and semen. Small amounts of the AIDS virus have recently been found in cervical or vaginal secretions of eight women in Boston and San Francisco studies but there is as yet no evidence that women can spread the disease to men during sexual intercourse. It is also not yet known whether several sexual or IV-drug-related exposures or just one is required in contracting AIDS. Nor is it known what factors, including stress, previous infections, or genetic susceptibility, may contribute to acquiring the disease.

The incidence of AIDS rose from 2,600 cases in 1983 to 17,871 recorded cases, of whom 9,463 have died, as of March 3, 1986. Seventy-three percent were homosexual or bisexual men, and 17 percent were intravenous drug users who may have shared needles. Hemophiliacs who contracted the disease through use of the blood clotting Factor VIII constitute 0.6 percent of AIDS cases. (A newly developed blood test became available in April 1985 to protect persons requiring blood transfusions and blood banks are considered safe. Hemophiliacs receiving their first blood transfusions after April 1985 are now protected.) Other victims are children born to female AIDS patients. The small number of female victims (7 percent of all AIDS cases) in the United States are either intravenous drug users themselves or sexual partners of drug users. The patterns of transmission have been stable for five years and most experts expect little change. The incidence of AIDS outside these risk groups is extremely low, about one in a million people. Female prostitutes in the United States thus far have not been found to transmit the disease through sexual activity although it must be remembered that many are IV drug users.

Between 700,000 and 1.4 million people have been exposed to the disease and are asymptomatic carriers of the virus, including 17–67 percent of all gay and bisexual men, 50–87 percent of intravenous drug users, 72–85 percent of hemophiliacs who received clotting factor before March 1985 and 5–40 percent of female street prostitutes, many of whom are drug users. Of these, a still unknown proportion will develop full-blown AIDS, and others will develop symptoms like ARC, a mild version of the disease. (Some people suffer from ARC for years, others seem to recover, and anywhere from 5–30 percent develop AIDS within five years, depending on which studies are cited.) Many others may continue in the carrier state. One patient thus far has been known to revert back to normal. All of those exposed may be infectious to others but only under the specific conditions described below. Little is known about the long-range effects of exposure, since the virus appears to incubate in the body for two to five or more years before the disease appears.

There is no current cure for AIDS; one treats the symptoms and keeps patients in the active stages of the disease as comfortable as possible. But changes in certain sexual behaviors can greatly reduce the risk of contracting AIDS in the first place:

- Avoid sexual contact with persons who have active AIDS and un-protected sex with AIDS virus carriers.
- Sexual monogamy (one consistent partner), or greatly limiting the number of sexual partners, reduces chances of exposure to AIDS. Casual sex is considered far riskier than in the past.
- Use condoms and diaphragms along with spermicidal jellies, creams, and foams (some evidence suggests that spermicides may help pro-tect against the virus). Outside the body, the AIDS virus is easily killed with common soaps, detergents, and household cleansers, or water at the temperature of 133 degrees or higher. (However, once inside, the virus is highly immune, even to powerful drugs.)
- Be careful about unprotected anal intercourse, and possibly oral-genital sexual activity and deep kissing, since cuts, sores, or tears in these locations give the AIDS virus access to the bloodstream. Anal intercourse itself can cause injury or tears in body tissue, leaving the person vulnerable to AIDS infection.
- Women who are menstruating should particularly avoid sexual contact with bisexual men, since the women are thought to be more vulnerable to infection during menstruation.
- Consider taking vitamin C. Some leading scientists believe five hun-dred milligrams of vitamin C daily may help in maintaining the body's immune system.

Although research efforts have intensified, an effective vaccine to prevent AIDS is thought to be at least five years away. Researchers are also looking for cures for those already infected. Until success is achieved, the only control over the spread of AIDS will be public information and self-protective sexual conduct, especially the avoid-ance of unprotected anal and oral intercourse and contact with multiple sex partners among high-risk groups. Much has already been done in terms of self-protection by gay and bisexual men. It has been more difficult to convince IV drug users to protect them-selves, but one immediate direction might be the provision of free sterile disposable needles.

Most cities now have centers and services that can offer in-

ing birth may die or suffer permanent neurological damage. Women with the disease are at greater risk for cervical cancer.

Symptoms appear in the form of itching and small, painful "sores" or lesions in the genital area four to seven days after sexual contact. Flu-like symptoms may be present, as well as general fatigue. Symptoms often disappear, only to recur. Most persons with the disease have three or four flare-ups a year, each lasting several days to three weeks. The disease is most highly contagious during this time.

If blisters or lesions do occur, they are treated with a cleansing salt solution. Secondary infections may be treated or avoided by use of oral sulfanamides. Though there is currently neither a cure nor a prevention for genital herpes, a new antiviral drug, acyclovir (Zovirax), introduced in 1984, can prevent flare-ups of the disease. Flare-ups may recur if the medication is stopped. Long-term side effects of acyclovir, if any, are unknown. Research is under way for a vaccine to prevent the disease.

Genital herpes was once described as the "leprosy of the 1980s," but much of the panic has subsided, due both to the introduction of acyclovir and to growing awareness of the much greater threat of AIDS. Those who have herpes do admit to anxiety about telling potential partners they carry the disease. But most view herpes as a periodically annoying illness rather than as a cause for alarm and have learned to live with it.

GONORRHEA

Two million people or more contracted gonorrhea in 1984. Men typically show obvious symptoms two to fourteen days after infection, with a tingling sensation in the urethra, and shortly thereafter, pain during urination and a discharge from the penis. In women, the disease is asymptomatic for weeks and even months about 80 percent of the time. When symptoms do occur, they are a vaginal discharge and/or pain on urination, or frequency of urination. Gonorrhea can cause inflammation in the Fallopian tubes, resulting in infertility. Homosexual men may also be symptomless for a period of time, with the infection residing in the throat or rectum.

Antibiotics are the usual treatment. Special drugs, like cloxacillin and spectinomycin, are used for the rapidly increasing cases (a doubling of such cases in 1985) of penicillin-resistant strains of the disease. Patients are asked to refrain from sexual contact until they are cured, and all recent sexual contacts should be traced and treated as well. Retests are done until the doctor is certain the disease is cured.

SYPHILIS

Syphilis, once a dread disease, is now easily detectable and treatable in its early stages. Ninety thousand cases were treated in 1984. Syphilis is caused by an infectious organism that enters the lymph glands. If untreated, it can unfold over a period of years in three stages, the last of which is a fatal infection of the heart, brain, or other organ. Nearly all cases are now detected in the primary stage. Lesions (chancres or "sores") appear about four weeks after infection, or skin rashes in six to eight weeks. Penicillin is the antibiotic treatment for all three stages. Sexual activity must stop during treatment and all sexual contacts of the preceding three to twelve months should be identified and treated. Retests by the doctor are necessary until all traces of the disease have disappeared.

CHLAMYDIA

Chlamydia is the most common of all STDs, with three million new cases a year. It is an insidious disease, since 70 percent of infected women and 25 percent of men have no early symptoms. Many women discover it only after irreparable damage to their Fallopian tubes has occurred. If left untreated, chlamydia can cause pelvic inflammatory disease, tubal pregnancy, and infertility in women; lung and eye infections in babies born to infected mothers; and urethral infections and inflamed testes in men.

Detection has recently become easier through two new tests that can provide answers more cheaply and within hours, compared to the previous expensive test, which took four to six days. Even more accurate tests will soon be available. It is highly recommended that any woman who has new or varied sexual partners be tested regularly for chlamydia every six months. Women who are on birth control pills who have even slight vaginal discharge, urethral discomfort, urinary frequency, or dull lower abdominal or pelvic pain should be tested. Once the diagnosis is made, chlamydia is easily treated with ten to fourteen days of antibiotics such as tetracycline or erythromycin (not penicillin).

The early detection and treatment that have been and essentially still are the solution for gonorrhea, syphilis, and most recently chlamydia, are inapplicable to diseases like genital herpes and especially AIDS. The sole protection against such currently incurable diseases is prevention from contracting the disease in the first place. Earlier we outlined recommended sexual behaviors to lessen the risk of exposure to AIDS, especially the avoidance of unprotected anal intercourse. In the meantime, research efforts must continue to be directed toward learning how to control this dangerous and deadly new public health threat that endangers a significant portion of the male population.

5

FOR MEN: DIAGNOSIS AND TREATMENT OF PHYSICALLY CAUSED IMPOTENCE

WHAT IS IMPOTENCE?

In this chapter we will refer to impotence as erectile dysfunction—that is, the loss of a man's ability to obtain an erection sufficient to achieve or maintain sexual intercourse. (The terms "impotence" and "erection problem" will be used interchangeably.) Rarely do men lose totally the capacity for at least some degree of erection; most have "erection problems," which interfere with full sexual expression. The severity of impotence ranges from being incapable of total erection some of the time to incapacity most or all of the time. Impotence also refers to the inability to sustain an erection even if one is initially able to have one. It is estimated that about ten million American men—one out of eight—suffer from chronic erection problems or impotence. This is *not* part of the normal physical process of growing older even though problems increase with age, due to physical illness and other causes. If impotence regularly occurs, one should investigate the cause or causes and treat the condition. Many cases—perhaps the majority—can be improved or even reversed with proper diagnosis and treatment. Therefore it is imperative for a man to be examined medically first to determine whether or not a physical condition is acting as a partial or complete cause of his impotence.

WHAT PRODUCES AN ERECTION?

The physiology and psychology of getting and maintaining an erection are complicated and are based on reflexes rather than consciously controlled by the man himself. Two sets of messages—stimulation of the penis through touch and/or stimulation of the brain through erotic thoughts triggered by sights, smells, hearing, fantasies, or memories—are sent to nerve centers in the spinal cord. These nerve centers send messages to the pelvic blood vessels, causing them to enlarge and fill with blood (engorge), creating an erection. Some believe special valves in the penis close to retain engorgement. Testosterone and chemicals known as neurotransmitters play an important but still unclear role. Mental stimulation alone is often enough to produce erections in adolescents and very young men. But most men in their late forties and their fifties need at least some tactile stimulation of the penis, in addition to erotic thoughts, before erection occurs.

AT WHAT AGE ARE ERECTION PROBLEMS
LIKELY TO OCCUR?

There has been little reliable scientific information concerning the actual experience of impotence as men grow older. Kinsey documented a decline in potency with age up until the age of fifty, but his sample over fifty was too small to draw conclusions from. Duke University and the Gerontology Research Center of the National Institute on Aging in Baltimore have found a general pattern of decline as well, but with much individual variation. Indeed, a significant proportion of men had stable and even rising patterns of sexual activity with age. For our purposes here, it is clear that erection problems do increase with age (due to illness or other causes—but not due to physical aging itself); however, they are not inevitable, nor are they by any means always permanent.

THE MIND-BODY ISSUE IN IMPOTENCE

It has long been generally accepted that at least 90 percent of impotence in men over sixty was psychologically based, with only about 10 percent physiologically caused. These figures, quoted since the 1920s, can be traced back to the book *Impotence in the Male*, by one of Freud's colleagues, William Stekel. William Masters and Virginia Johnson, pioneer sex researchers, arrived at the same conclusions in their laboratory studies of older men, and psychotherapists and sex counselors since have promulgated these beliefs. The proportion of psychologically based impotence among men forty to sixty has been estimated to be even higher, at 95 percent. However, more effective diagnostic techniques and a growing understanding of the physiology of impotence are changing those views. In the last few years, biomedical researchers, using a variety of more sophisticated measurements and advanced techniques, including sleep studies, have begun to suspect that impotence may have a much higher physiological component, perhaps involving 50 percent of all cases of impotence (five million men), regardless of age. The rates may be even higher for older men, especially those with vascular problems.

In this book, we have made an artificial division between physically based and psychologically based impotence, to facilitate discussion. In truth the two are usually intermixed, with a greater emphasis in one direction or another. The psychological aspects of impotence are discussed in other chapters.

MAJOR CAUSES OF PHYSICALLY BASED IMPOTENCE

In a significant number of cases of impotence, it is likely that physical illness has been undetected or at least that a mixed diagnosis involving physical as well as emotional components has been overlooked. This helps to explain the estimated 60 percent or higher failure rate from using psychotherapy alone to treat potency problems. The major causes of the approximately five million cases of primarily physically based impotence are listed here:

PHYSICAL PROBLEM	CASES OF IMPOTENCE (APPROXIMATE)
Diabetes mellitus	2,000,000 (or more)
Vascular insufficiency (arteriosclerosis, hypertension, antihypertensive medications [beta blocker agents])	1,500,000
Radical surgery (prostatectomies, colostomies, cystectomies, etc.)	650,000
Trauma (spinal cord injuries, pelvic fractures, etc.)	400,000
Hypogonadism and other endocrine disorders	300,000
Multiple sclerosis	180,000
Peyronie's disease (fibrous cavernitis)	Unknown
Side effects from medications (estrogens, anticholinergic drugs, excessive tranquilizers, antidepressants, antihypertensive agents, opiates, alcohol, etc.)	Unknown

DIAGNOSTIC PROCEDURES

HISTORY TAKING

Both the patient and his partner should provide a history of their past sex life together, along with a description of the current problem and a list of prior treatments. The quality of the patient's personal relationships should be assessed, as should financial, family, social, and environmental difficulties. Any possible psychiatric problems and direct psychological contributors to the impotence require assessment. The medical history includes a review of occupational hazards, alcohol and drug use, systemic illnesses such as diabetes or cirrhosis, neurologic or vascular disease, pelvic surgery, radiation trauma, muscle strength and endurance, genitourinary infections or obstructions, changes in secondary sex characteristics, headaches or visual disturbance, and endocrine gland function.

It is becoming increasingly clear how complicated impotence can be and how careful doctors must be in evaluating it. For example, evidence from the ongoing Baltimore Longitudinal Study of Aging suggests that visual stimulation—sexual arousal caused by what one sees—may be influenced by vascular, neural, or endocrine changes in the brain or by simple changes in the eye itself, with a resulting inability to translate visual stimuli to erotic arousal.

PHYSICAL EXAMINATION

In addition to the usual physical examination, the physician should concentrate on detecting abnormalities, including any in the external sex organs and secondary sex characteristics such as hair growth. Possible problems in circulation and in the central or peripheral nervous system are also areas of focus.

SLEEP STUDIES

Sleep studies have produced an extremely useful diagnostic measurement called nocturnal penile tumescence (NPT), the monitoring of erections during sleep.* It is known that healthy men have erections approximately every ninety minutes throughout the night (during REM, or dreaming, sleep) and that each episode lasts some twenty to twenty-five minutes. Measurement of the circumference of the tip and base of the penis of a man during sleep over a period of three nights, together with encephalographic recording of sleep patterns and observations of eye movements, generally indicate whether the capacity for full or partial erection exists. (There appears to be a parallel phenomenon in women, with vaginal lubrication and engorgement of the pelvic area, although there are few studies to confirm this.) Minimal erections or the absence of erections during sleep strongly suggests but does not definitely prove an organic basis for impotence.

The NPT measurement can prevent not only the misuse of long-term psychotherapy as the sole treatment for impotence of organic or physical origin, but also unnecessary diagnostic examinations, medical treatment, and surgery for impotence with purely

---

*NPT was first described in 1944 by Ohlmeyer and associates. It received no further attention until the 1960s, when "sleep labs" began developing in the United States, including those at Mount Sinai Medical Center in New York City and the Menninger Clinic in Topeka, Kansas. A portable home monitoring device has also been developed. For information on clinics contact Association of Sleep Disorder Centers, Sleep Research Center Department of Psychiatry and Behavioral Science, Stanford University School of Medicine, Stanford, CA 94305.

psychological causes. NPT does not, however, explain the probable nature of the organic impairment. For this a fuller physical evaluation is needed. An abnormal NPT should prompt a physician to recommend the following examinations:

- Urological—to study the genitals and bladder function.
- Neurological—to look for signs of trauma and neuropathy.
- Endocrinological—to check testosterone and other hormone levels.
- Vascular—checking the pelvic area, especially for penile blood pressure and pulse.

Since NPT is a relatively new procedure, several observations are in order:

- NPT measures only the circumference, not the firmness, of an erection. Since a penis can be fully inflated but still not rigid, NPT is not a complete indicator of penile function.
- Normal NPT appears to decrease slightly but consistently with age, but healthy older men have not been widely studied. Normal erectile patterns may become more erratic with age both at night and during the day. For example, older men typically have more sleep disturbances and changes in sleeping patterns compared to those younger. The impact of sleep and age has not been studied with respect to NPT testing.
- It is believed that REM stage sleep is necessary for NPT to occur. Certain hypnotic and other psychoactive drugs can suppress REM sleep and may produce a false reading of REM-related NPT. They may also affect night erections. (Anxiety may have a similar effect, through the suppression of dreaming.) For patients who drink heavily or use drugs, a second NPT test should be done two to four weeks after drugs or several months after alcohol has been stopped.
- Men with severe vascular or neurologic disease may have firm nighttime erections of brief duration even though they are essentially impotent the remainder of the time.
- Under conditions of study in a sleep laboratory, some men may have abnormal NPT results.

Some physicians recommend a "postage stamp test" as a simple screening device before NPT monitoring. A ring of postage stamps pasted around the penis before sleep will be broken if an erection occurs during sleep. (The wearing of briefs helps keep the stamps in place.) This is not a very reliable test, since the stamps can be broken through movement during sleep. It also does not measure the circumference at both the tip and the base, as does the NPT. But it is simple and harmless, and may offer reassurance if the stamps are consistently broken during sleep. A somewhat more reliable "snap gauge" uses a Velcro strip which encircles the penis. It consists of three bands, which break at various different degrees of penile rigidity. A third device now becoming available is called a "regiscon" and is used to measure hardness of a penis as well as circumference.

OTHER DIAGNOSTIC TESTS

Other methods of diagnostic testing of impotence are visual stimulation, such as sexually explicit pictures or movies, the use of a vibrator, and a papaverine injection directly into the penis. Papaverine will produce an erection that lasts three to four hours if a patient who is sexually excited is also physiologically normal. (This can be very effective psychologically, showing a patient with psychological impotence that he can have an erection.) Penile blood pressure measurements may be useful, as well as a glucose tolerance test to rule diabetes in or out. Penile blood pressure measurements are increasingly employed in diagnosing other erectile disorders as well. Procedures such as thermography of the penis (measuring penile skin temperature to detect changes in surface blood flow) and pelvic arteriography (x ray of arteries after a dye has been injected into the blood stream) are in experimental use.

TREATMENT OF IMPOTENCE

MEDICAL TREATMENTS

In addition to treatment of specific underlying diseases, as outlined in the previous chapter, impotence can occasionally be treated successfully with hormones. At present, male hormone therapy (sex steroid replacement) is controversial and experimental. Replacement of the male hormone testosterone has little known permanent beneficial effect on the sexual problems of men, particularly impotence, unless there is definitely proved testicular deficiency in the production of male hormones—such as in hypogonadism, a rare condition. Although his studies have not been replicated, endocrinologist Robert Greenblatt, of the Medical College of Georgia, is more optimistic about the effectiveness and safety of testosterone therapy for impotence, particularly when the hormone is administered intramuscularly (by injection) in a specified regimen. Any benefit from testosterone should show up in three to four weeks, but even in those men who appear to respond to such treatment, improvement is generally short-lived and may be a positive placebo response rather than a true physiological one, except in clear-cut deficiencies. There may be side effects with large hormone dosages, such as fluid retention, excess red blood cells, a lowered sperm count, jaundice, or even breast enlargement. Evidence indicates that testosterone may stimulate already existing prostatic growth; thus it should not be given if the prostate gland is enlarged. Doctor and patient must weigh risks against possible benefits, but caution is recommended.

Currently, no medication can safely be prescribed to correct vascular-disease-related impotence; but studies under way suggest that drugs may be produced that could be injected directly into the penis to improve blood flow. In one highly experimental study by urologist Adrian Zorgniotti at the New York University School of Medicine, a vasoactive, smooth-muscle-relaxing substance (papaverine hydrochloride) together with an alpha blocker (phentolamine mesylate) is injected into the corpora cavernosa of the penis, two cylinders that hold blood through the mechanism of thousands of tiny valves. This increases penile blood flow, allowing the patient to achieve an erection that lasts long enough to permit intercourse. Results are reported to be satisfactory to excellent, with intercourse possible about twice a week although only a few men have been studied. Complications have included brief loss of feeling in the penis and difficulty reaching orgasm and ejaculation. One patient developed a prolonged erection (priapism) that required treatment. Other short-term and long-term effects of papaverine injection are not yet known.

Nerve damage to the penis as the result of spinal cord injury, lumbar disk disease, radical pelvic surgery, multiple sclerosis, or juvenile-onset diabetes can cause impotence by impeding blood flow. Boston University Medical Center urologist Irwin Goldstein has treated such cases by injecting combined papaverine hydrochloride and phentolamine mesylate into the penis. Twenty patients were able to return to normal sexual intercourse, including ejaculation. Prolonged erections were a side effect with some hypertensive individuals.

Zinc deficiency in the daily diet may interfere with normal hormone production and therefore affect sexual functioning. Zinc is found in most foods and the recommended daily allowance (RDA) is only fifteen milligrams per day, but if a rare deficiency is found, zinc can be easily obtained in shellfish, seafood, meats, and certain whole grains, nuts, and legumes, or in multiple vitamins. It is interesting that oysters, long recommended as aphrodisiacs, have one of the highest concentrations of zinc found in food.

Exciting research is under way on hormonal and neurohormonal aspects of impotence. A substance called vasoactive intestinal polypeptide (VIP) was found to be depleted in the penises of twenty-eight impotent diabetic men. More accurately, the VIP-containing nerves were depleted. Evidence indicates that VIP may be the principal nerve transmitter involved in penile erection—an important piece of basic information, if true, and one that could lead to greater understanding of the physiology of organic impotence.

SURGERY

PROSTHESES   Specific surgical procedures to treat impotence are under study and have been used on limited numbers of American men (about thirty thousand), mostly in the last five to ten years. Permanent penile prostheses or implants have been inserted in cases of permanent organic impotence, especially those due to diabetes, and in a few instances where psychological impotence has not responded to psychotherapy. The prosthesis serves mainly to enhance the patient's self-esteem and possibly improve his partner's pleasure. It does not in itself produce a climax for the man or increase sexual desire. However, those men who could have an orgasm before surgery can do so afterward. If they are capable of an ejaculation (and a prosthesis does not interfere with ejaculation), such men can also father children.

The four main manufacturers of prostheses are American Medical Systems, Surgiteck, Mentor, and Dacomed, all of Minneapolis. They will provide information about their products in response to letters or calls.

The *Scott inflatable prosthesis*, developed in 1973, is a hydraulic device that is totally implanted with a saline fluid reservoir and a two-cylinder balloon-like device inside the penis's corpora cavernosa. The erection is initiated by squeezing a pump in the scrotum above one of the testicles. This releases saline solution from the reservoir through the action of a subcutaneous pump. Another part of the pump drains the fluid after intercourse. Major advantages to this device are that the partner may be unaware of its presence and the diameter (not the length) of the erection is fully controllable. However, the penis does not feel as "hard" to the touch as with a normal erection. Other disadvantages are that there are mechanical failures in about 10–30 percent of cases. Removal of the defective portion and insertion of a new component is then necessary.

A second inflatable prosthesis is made by the Mentor Company, using polyurethane rather than silicone for its basic construction. The pump is slightly stronger than with the Scott inflatable device and costs are similar. A third inflatable prosthesis is manufactured by American Medical Systems and Surgiteck.

The *Small-Carrion semi-rigid rod prosthesis*, developed in 1975, is a pliable silicon rod with a silicon sponge interior which is inserted in each of the two corpus cavernosum of the penis, creating a permanent erection. In the past it was the most commonly used prosthesis, more than 20,000 having been implanted. (Other prostheses are more likely to be used today.) Among its advantages are that it is simple, relatively easy to implant, and less expensive than an inflatable implant. When not in use, the penis with its prosthesis is ordinarily bent down into an athletic supporter or bent upward against the abdomen and held in place with an abdominal binder. Disadvantages are that the partner is aware of it, and it may have a tendency to buckle or bend in her vagina. The erection size is determined by the rods and cannot be varied; it is usually smaller than the original erection size. The tip of the penis will droop somewhat. The implant may cause irritation from rubbing against clothes all day; injury to the soft tissue of the penis may result. Because of its size the prosthesis can interfere with athletic activities. It may also cause problems in performing some urological tests or examinations.

The *Flexi-rod II prosthesis* is a modification of the Small-Carrion device, with a hinge that allows the penis to be bent downward more easily when not in use. Some patients find that it is less stable for intercourse than the Small-Carrion prosthesis although stability has been improved.

The *Jonas silicon-silver prosthesis*, perhaps the most widely used prosthesis, is also similar to the Small-Carrion device, but contains a central core of braided silver wire. This allows the penis to be held rather firmly in any position and it can more easily be bent out of the way. The silver core adds to the expense, however, and after a period of time the wires occasionally wear out and break.

Men with the following conditions are not considered good candidates for penile prosthesis:

- Untreated acute and severe depression. The depression should be successfully treated first.
- Serious psychosis or brain disease.
- Severe personality disorders, including the chronically dissatisfied.
- Severe and complicated marital problems.
- Impotence that is not clearly organic.
- Health conditions that contraindicate elective surgery.

When might a man and his doctor decide to try penile implant surgery? The following conditions are guidelines in reaching a decision. The advisability of surgery is commensurate with the number of conditions that are fulfilled.

- When it is very clear that the impotence is primarily a chronic organic problem, rather than strictly psychogenic. Examples of such organic problems are diabetes, vascular disease, problems from certain types of rectal or prostate surgery, pelvic nerve injury, spinal cord injury, and other traumas.
- When sexual desire is strong and intercourse is greatly valued by both partners.

- When there is evidence of continuing sexual activity between the partners even in the absence of sexual intercourse.
- When the presence of impotence per se is having a destructive effect on the relationship.
- When the couple have a realistic understanding of what may be achieved and both approve of the surgery. For example, in the process of deciding about surgery, men may falsely assume their partners are frustrated with the absence of intercourse or prefer intercourse to other methods of sexual activity. In fact, some partners with little interest in sex may not welcome their mate's new potency. Others may enjoy other forms of sexual activity more than intercourse.

The inclusion of partners in pre- and postsurgical evaluations is increasingly seen as important. Sex counseling in addition to surgery may be helpful, since couples often need explicit instruction on how best to use a prosthesis. If the female partner has been sexually inactive before her partner's surgery, she may need help with the dyspareunia or pain that can come from resumption of sexual activity or from the prosthesis itself. Kegel exercises may be recommended for conditioning the vaginal muscles to accommodate partners with the smaller and more flexible rod-type implants.

Risk factors for all implants involve the danger of a slight risk of infection at the time of insertion and mechanical malfunction with inflatable devices. In spite of this, estimates of current surgical success in implants is reported as high as 90 percent. However, patient and partner satisfaction may be significantly lower than this, particularly over time. Little is known about psychosocial adjustment or frequency of intercourse after surgery. Follow-up studies, when they have been done, are likely to check only on surgical results and possible complications rather than psychological and functional satisfaction levels.

Women may harbor fears of the risk of prosthesis surgery on their partners or of penile or vaginal injury during intercourse. There are a few reports of cases of sexual refusal and divorce following penile implant. The partners in these cases were obviously not eager to resume sexual relations and very likely had not given their consent for the surgery.

Some men have used their implants only for extramarital sexual activity, indicating unresolved problems in their primary relationship. In some cases, men have surgery for cosmetic reasons alone. A clue to this is patients' reports that the implant was not used for sexual activity by the time of the six-months postsurgery follow-up.

Some question the use of permanent prostheses at all, believing that sexual counseling could help couples find sexual satisfaction with techniques other than vaginal penetration by the penis. Helping men to learn to enjoy their partners' sexual pleasure and to derive their own sexual self-esteem from sources other than an erect penis are examples of these techniques. Such men concentrate on becoming expert and sensitive sexual partners. But we recognize that for other men, as well as their partners, an erect penis is a critical symbol of manhood and sex without intercourse is not the "real thing." For these men a penile prosthesis may be one solution to their anxieties and frustrations.

The use of a permanent prosthesis for psychologically rather than physically based impotence is another matter entirely. Surgery in these cases is usually considered questionable. The possibility, however remote, for spontaneous recovery is destroyed permanently if the penis has been structurally altered. Furthermore, the prosthesis may do little to change the man's emotional relationship with his partner and thus the situation may not be really improved. And finally, there are many kinds of therapy for sexual problems. A thorough trial of sex therapy with a skilled specialist is the generally recommended course of action when the patient does not respond to sympathetic listening or more traditional psychotherapy. If a man with psychogenic impotence has not recovered during a reasonable period of treatment, the possibility that it may be due to the wrong therapy or the wrong therapist must always be considered.

REVASCULARIZATION Revascularization is surgery involving the shifting of blood vessels. Used to restore normal blood circulation to the penis, it is still in the experimental stage, but shows promise. The procedure, which employs several different techniques, is not yet considered reliable; many patients' arteries have closed off again in one to fifteen months. Experiments in revascularization of the penis continue, largely because revascularization has become so successful in heart disease.

Arteriosclerosis and conditions such as peripheral vascular

disease, sickle cell anemia, traumas or accidents to the penis and surrounding areas, or simply an insufficient blood flow to the penis since birth can affect blood circulation to the penis, although it is unclear just what degree of vascular insufficiency will cause problems. In some cases men as young as twenty or thirty can have arteriosclerosis severe enough to impede full penile blood flow.

The evaluation process for penile revascularization, which usually involves taking an arteriogram, is generally used only when it helps document the presence of arteriosclerosis, when it is thought that a reconstructible lesion (often resulting from an accident) can be found, and when the patient strongly objects to a prosthesis, preferring a more physiological solution. Noninvasive diagnostic techniques, like the measurement of penile blood pressure, can also help to identify vascular insufficiency. Another diagnostic procedure, corpora cavernosography, is considered safe when done in specialized medical centers.

Revascularization is almost never recommended for diabetic impotence. Some surgeons feel revascularization is not indicated if the person has advanced general arteriosclerosis. Major risk factors of developing arteriosclerosis are hypertension, heavy smoking, and diabetes. Others believe that arteriosclerosis often advances segmentally, and if it is more advanced in the penis than in other parts of the body, revascularization in that area may result in many more years of functioning. In one vascular condition, Leriche's syndrome, there is an intermittent reduction of the penile blood supply needed for erection. Aching, fatigue, weakness, cramping, numbness, discomfort in the thigh, pain in the calf, or limping may accompany this syndrome. Many of the symptoms are relieved by rest. Surgery can eliminate the limp and also restore sexual potency.

VACUUM-CONSTRICTION DEVICES (V-C)

Vacuum-constriction devices for obtaining and maintaining erection are being tested by researchers such as urologist Perry Nadig of the University of Texas Medical School in San Antonio. A plastic-cylinder vacuum device is fitted over the unerect penis, a piece of plastic tubing is attached to an opening in the end of the device, and a gentle vacuum is produced by sucking out the air with a syringe or with one's mouth. The vacuum encourages blood flow into the penis, creating an erection. Once a full erection occurs, a wide rubber band stored on the end of the cylinder nearest the base of the penis is slipped around the penis to retain the blood there, maintaining the erection. The half-inch-wide rubber band must be the correct circumference to allow blood flow into the penis and yet hold enough blood in place to keep the erection. Use of the band is restricted to half an hour. If any pain or numbness occurs, the band should be removed immediately. The cost, which includes evaluation of the impotence problem and screening of the device for safety with each patient, is expected to be under $1,500. Compared to an implant, this method requires no surgery, it is much less expensive, and the penis is not permanently altered. Diabetic men, who are at greater risk of infection from surgery, may be especially good prospects for these devices. Of course, the V-C device is relatively new and untested (only 150 men have been studied); in addition, one's partner will be aware of its use and it requires preparation before sexual activity.

APHRODISIACS AND OTHER TREATMENTS

Because impotence is such a widespread concern, a host of questionable treatments have evolved. Folklore is full of reputed "remedies." Doctors have been known to prescribe herbs, greens, and massive amounts of vitamins B_{12} and E. There are also "youth doctors" and nonmedical entrepreneurs who produce and sell countless substances and gadgets advertised to rejuvenate sexual potency. People over forty, already worrying about signs of aging, are particular targets of fraudulent consumer schemes and devices that promise to "make you look younger" and "guarantee" prevention or cure of impotence. The U.S. Postal Service has provided us with a representive list of worthless nostrums or alleged aphrodisiacs.* Among them are Mexican Spanish Fly in Liquid Form, Instant Love Potion, Sex Stimulant for Women, Mad Dog Weed, Magic Lure, Super Nature Tablets, European Love Drops, and Linga Pendulum Penis Enlarger and Strengthener. New items on the market are Big Ox, made of vitamins and minerals, and VBE-21, advertised as the

---

*The Postal Service, by means of a charge of false representation in violation of Title 39, U.S. Code 30005, can bring action against person(s) engaged in promoting a scheme or device in order to obtain money or property through the mails.

"Doctor's Pill for Loss of Sex Drive." We have tabulated by popular and scientific names a variety of alleged aphrodisiacs. Watch out for them. If they seem to work, it is only through the power of suggestion, and any "cure" is likely to be temporary. Some are extremely dangerous; Spanish fly can kill.

SOME FALSE APHRODISIACS

Alcohol	Especially wine
Cantharidin	Tincture of *Cantharis vesicatoria* (Spanish fly)
Capsicum	Extract of *Capsicum frutescens* (cayenne pepper from South America)
Cimicifugin	Resin from *Cimicifuga racemosa* (black snakeroot)
Cubeb	Oleoresin from *Piper cubeba* (from Java)
Damiana	Dried leaves of *Turnera diffusa* (from Mexico)
Ergot	Alkaloids from *Claviceps purpurea*
Marijuana	*Cannabis sativa*
Nux vomica	Extract from seeds of *Strychnos nux-vomica*
Sanguinaria	Extract from *Sanguinaria canadensis* (bloodroot)
Vitamin E	di-Alpha-tocopherol

Representatives of the federal Food and Drug Administration (FDA) state that no plant or animal materials have been demonstrated to be either safe or effective as aphrodisiacs. The use of powdered rhinoceros horn has had the additional tragic consequence of endangering an entire species of animal. The FDA began an attempt to ban the sale of all nonprescription aphrodisiacs as of mid-1985.

The ban does not, however, cover products, like ginseng, that do not claim to be aphrodisiacs but nevertheless have that association in the public mind. Chinese ginseng (*Panax quinquefolium*) has been used for at least two thousand years in the belief that it preserves health, increases alertness, and improves endurance. The aphrodisiac action of ginseng has been interpreted (but not scientifically proven) to be a consequence of improved health, which produces a return to normal sexual desire and functioning. Taken in moderation, such as half a teaspoon of ginseng powder in a cup of hot water three times a day, ginseng has no known adverse side effects. Very large doses may cause problems like insomnia or anxiety. The supposed positive effects of ginseng are said to occur gradually over a period of months. Ginseng is readily available in health food stores.

One aphrodisiac that may at least partially live up to its reputation and eventually graduate to the role of a tested drug is yohimbine, an extract from the bark of the African yohimbe tree. Physicians at Queen's University Medical School in Canada report that yohimbine was used in a study of twenty-three men, ten of whom experienced improved potency. Yohimbine, an alpha blocker, induces dilation of certain blood vessels in the penis. It also increases release of norepinephrine, a substance that is helpful in producing erections.

The body itself may manufacture aphrodisiacs, particularly amphetamines and opiate-like substances. These may play a role in attracting human beings to each other, arousing sexual desire, and helping to maintain strong attachment. Some consider a chemical that comes from the hypothalamus, the central portion of the brain, to be the ultimate aphrodisiac. This luteinizing hormone–releasing hormone (LHRH) has been shown, in animal studies, to function as a stimulant of sexual activity even after the sex glands have been removed. This effect suggests that the action occurs directly in the brain itself.

SELF-HELP ORGANIZATIONS

A self-help organization, Impotents Anonymous (IA), with headquarters at 5119 Bradley Boulevard, Chevy Chase, MD 20815 (phone 301-656-3649), offers a network of support involving men who have impotence problems as well as those whose impotence has been corrected. Critics of the organization contend that it focuses heavily on prosthesis implants at the expense of other treatments. Ninety percent of the eighty IA chapter coordinators have had implants. IA itself maintains that its approach is one of "total care," including medical, psychiatric, and self-help methods. IA keeps an up-to-date referral list of physicians and therapists who specialize in potency problems. I-ANON, patterned after the AL-ANON program in Alcoholic Anonymous, is a support group for the partners of men with potency problems. Bruce and Eileen MacKenzie, who founded both organizations after their own experience with impotence, state: "Impotence is where alcoholism was thirty years ago. Ten million men have been in the closet and we are helping them get out."

6

FOR WOMEN: ESTROGEN ANXIETY AND MENOPAUSAL SYMPTOMS

WHY WOMEN ARE ANXIOUS ABOUT ESTROGEN
REPLACEMENT THERAPY (ERT)

Estrogen, a natural body hormone, was first artificially produced in the 1930s and by the 1960s it was a highly popular method of treatment for the discomforts of menopause, including sexual discomforts. Fueled by the enthusiasm of both physicians and their patients, and by books like Robert Wilson's *Feminine Forever* (1966), estrogen in its most popular form, Premarin, became the fifth most commonly used drug by 1975. (Premarin, produced by Ayerst Laboratories, accounted for over 80 percent of all estrogen prescriptions filled.) About one half of American women at or past menopause were taking it. Estrogen was promoted as a protection against hot flashes, vaginal atrophy, heart disease, depression, lowered sex drive, osteoporosis, cancer, and general aging signs like wrinkles and gray hair. Some thought it especially protected against breast cancer. The only known and common side effects from estrogen use were thought to be occasional dose-related uterine bleeding and minor complaints of nausea, fluid retention, weight gain, and increased susceptibility to vaginal yeast infections.

Estrogen replacement therapy became the subject of anxious public and professional debate in 1976, when it was found to be associated with a somewhat increased risk of endometrial, or uterine, cancer. Links between estrogen and endometrial cancer had been made since the 1940s, but five studies in 1975–76 showed definitively that estrogen replacement therapy was associated with a five to fifteen times increased risk of endometrial cancer, especially if estrogen was taken more than one year. The use of menopausal hormones declined dramatically in the next few years. However, with the passage of time, estrogen use began to rise again as doctors became reassured about its safety under new guidelines for use, which included smaller and shorter-term dosages, often combined with progestin, and greater clarity about contraindications. For the circumstances under which estrogen should not be used at all or should be used with caution, see Table 1. A proportion of women and their doctors remain anxious about the risks, and unfortunately the weighing of risks and benefits must be done with a still incomplete scientific understanding of the many effects, short and long term, of estrogen use.

THE PRESENT STATE OF KNOWLEDGE—RISKS AND BENEFITS

With short-term use, estrogen replacement therapy can alleviate the usually temporary menopausal symptoms, such as hot flashes and night sweats. Longer use is for protection against vaginal atrophy and dryness and the bone loss of osteoporosis. A listing of possible benefits and risks has been provided in Table 2. A fuller discussion follows.

HOT FLASHES

About 25 percent of menopausal women have hot flashes of sufficient frequency and/or severity to cause them to seek medical attention. Estrogen therapy usually gives prompt and effective relief

---

Table 1 Possible Contraindications to the Use of Estrogen Replacement Therapy (ERT) Postmenopausally

ERT SHOULD ABSOLUTELY NOT BE GIVEN IF THE FOLLOWING ARE PRESENT:
• Estrogen-dependent cancer (for example, breast cancer)
• Undiagnosed vaginal bleeding
• Acute or chronic liver disease
• History of vascular thrombosis, embolism, stroke, or heart attack
• Allergies to estrogen in any form

CAUTION IS REQUIRED IF THE FOLLOWING ARE PRESENT:
• History of hypertension
• Fibrocystic breast disease
• Coronary heart disease
• Familial hyperlipidemia
• Migraine
• Epilepsy
• Endometriosis
• Abnormal pap smear or endometrial cellular atypia biopsy
• Diabetes mellitis
• Gall bladder disease
• Family history of breast or endometrial cancer
• Porphyria
• Fibroid tumor of the uterus
• Combination of obesity, varicose veins, and cigarette smoking

---

from hot flashes and sleep disorders arising from hot flash disturbance during the night. Not all women respond to therapy, for reasons that remain unclear. Others require much larger dosages than are usually given to obtain relief. In addition, up to 25 percent of women who seek medical relief from ERT receive the same relief from a placebo. The lowest effective dose of estrogen is determined by keeping a daily "flash count" that pinpoints the dosage at which frequency and severity of hot flashes are at an acceptable level.

VAGINAL ATROPHY

ERT is very effective in reversing atrophy of the vaginal wall (epithelium) and vaginal dryness, which can cause uncomfortable and at times painful intercourse, frequent urination, and even incontinence. It does not appear to improve relaxation of vaginal muscles. (Use of the Kegel exercise described on pages 113-14 can improve vaginal muscle tone.)

Table 2   Considerations in the Use of Estrogens for Treating the Menopausal Syndrome

POSSIBLE BENEFITS	POSSIBLE RISKS
Decrease in the frequency and/or severity of hot flashes and night sweats with attendant insomnia	Nausea, fluid retention, facial acne (for some)
Prevention or relief of atrophic vaginitis	Postmenopausal bleeding (requiring investigation)
Prevention or relief of atrophy of the vulva and atrophic urethritis	Increased severity of cystic breast disease
Prevention of thinning of the skin	Accelerated growth of preexisting uterine fibroid tumors
Prevention of osteoporosis*	Increased risk of gallstones (risk increased 2.5 times in one study)
Mental tonic effect	
[Evidence is emerging that the most significant possible benefit may be an overall decrease in mortality.—Authors]	Increased risk of uterine cancer†
	Increased risk of breast cancer‡
	Deep vein thrombophlebitis and thromboembolism§
	Increased blood pressure (rare)
	Decreased sugar tolerance (rare)

PRINCIPLES FOR THE USE OF ESTROGENS IN TREATING ESTROGEN-DEFICIENCY STATES

1. As each woman reaches the menopausal years (45 to 55) she should assess her own status and perceived needs. Next she should familiarize herself with the benefits and possible risks of estrogen replacement therapy. Then, if she thinks she needs medical guidance and/or treatment, she should discuss all aspects of her situation with her physician and share in the decision regarding the use of hormones.

2. A clear indication for the use of estrogen should exist. See Possible Benefits listed above. Estrogens do not retard the natural progression of general aging, and they should not be used in the hope of "preserving femininity."

3. Before estrogen therapy is started, appropriate examinations should be per-

*With long-term treatment.
†Risk increased only after 3 years of continuous use; risk increases progressively with increased dosage and duration of use and ranges from four- to eightfold.
‡ Existing data are controversial and contradictory. Some evidence suggests a possible increased risk but only after 3 or more years of continuous use of conjugated estrogens at a dosage of 1.25 mg daily.
§ Applies mostly to use of synthetic unconjugated steroid hormones (ethinyl estradiol and mestranol), and less likely to be related to conjugated equine estrogens, estradiol, or estriol given in customary dosage.

(Continued)

formed and due consideration given to the following possible contraindications to the use of estrogen:

- Pregnancy
- History of venous thrombosis or pulmonary embolism
- Present or previous cancer of the breast
- Cancer of the uterus
- Strong family history of breast or uterine cancer
- Current liver disease or previous cholestatic jaundice
- Chronic gall bladder disease, with or without stones
- Abnormal elevation of blood lipids (cholesterol, triglycerides, etc.)
- History of porphyria
- Large uterine fibroids
- Any estrogen-dependent tumor
- Combination of obesity, varicose veins, and cigarette smoking
- Diabetes mellitus
- Severe hypertension

4. In the young woman experiencing premature menopause (destruction or removal of both ovaries), the long-term use of estrogen replacement is justified, provided appropriate precautions are observed (see guidelines, page 77)

5. In the menopausal woman experiencing hot flashes and/or atrophic vaginitis, the *short-term* use of estrogen therapy is generally felt to be acceptable, with appropriate supervision and guidance. (Approximately 20% to 25% of menopausal women experience hot flashes of sufficient frequency and/or severity to warrant treatment.) Estrogen replacement therapy provides symptomatic relief; it is not a permanent cure for hot flashes.

6. *Long-term* estrogen therapy for *all* women after the menopause cannot be justified. Treatment must be carefully individualized (see guidelines, pages 78–79).

7. It is generally recommended that estrogens be taken cyclically. The customary schedule is from the 1st through the 25th day of each month, with no estrogen during the remaining days of the month. After 6 to 12 months of continuous use, the estrogen dose should be gradually reduced over a period of 2 to 3 months and then discontinued, to assess the individual's need for resumption of use.

8. The lowest effective daily dose of estrogen should be determined and maintained for the duration of the treatment.

9. Vaginal cream preparations of estrogen may be considered instead of orally administered estrogen if the only indication is atrophic vaginitis. However, it should be noted that these preparations allow rapid absorption of estrogen into the systemic circulation, and do not permit accurate control of dosage. They should be used intermittently and only as needed to correct the symptoms of atrophic vaginitis. (NOTE: The estrogen in vaginal creams can be absorbed through the skin of the penis and cause tenderness of the breast in men.)

10. The unnecessary prolongation of estrogen therapy should be avoided. It is advisable to use estrogens in the lowest effective dose and for only as long as necessary to relieve symptoms.

Reprinted from The Essential Guide to Prescription Drugs, *fourth edition, by James W. Long, M.D. (Harper & Row, 1985).*

EARLY MENOPAUSE

Unless it is medically contraindicated, most doctors recommend the use of ERT until age forty-five or fifty in women who have undergone natural or surgical premature menopause. This counteracts the effects of an abrupt surgically produced menopause and helps to create a more gentle transition.

OSTEOPOROSIS

ERT begun during or just after menopause and continued throughout life is thought to reduce the rapid bone loss that occurs postmenopausally and thereby also reduces the chances of hip, wrist, and arm fractures in later life. Osteoporosis indirectly causes fifteen thousand to thirty thousand deaths in later life among females yearly and the rate of disability is considerably higher. If ERT is discontinued, bone loss reportedly recurs and some believe it occurs at a pace more rapid than normal. (See Table 3, section III, no. 3.)

HEART DISEASE

A study of over two thousand women, reported in February 1983 in the *Journal of the American Medical Association*, suggests that postmenopausal women who take estrogen live longer than those who do not. This may be related to the fact that estrogen raises the blood levels of high-density-lipoprotein (HDL) cholesterol, a substance associated with reduced risk of heart disease. These findings are controversial, however. It is much more widely accepted that low-dose estrogen treatment of women after menopause causes neither an increase nor a decrease in atherosclerosis, coronary heart disease, or stroke.

HYPERTENSION

There is a well-known significant association between estrogen in birth control pills and increased incidence of hypertension. (The association is reversible when estrogen is discontinued.) But little is known about the effects on hypertension from low-dosage estrogen taken postmenopausally.

GALL BLADDER DISEASE

A significant increase in the incidence of gall bladder disease is reported among women who are on postmenopausal doses of conjugated estrogen.

BREAST DISEASE

The evidence associating ERT and breast cancer is inconclusive. However, the ability of estrogen to produce cancer in laboratory animals has been demonstrated repeatedly in the last fifty years in at least six animal species and in at least eight organ sites, including the breast. The length of time it can take before breast cancer reveals itself (from four to eight years) complicates the study of estrogen and breast cancer. Most doctors believe that women who are at high risk of developing breast cancer or who have benign or malignant breast disease should avoid estrogen use since it seems to stimulate some breast disease. However, controversy remains as to whether estrogen therapy itself increases the risk of developing breast disease. A number of well-designed studies thus far do not support this idea. Furthermore, a study by Gambrell at the Medical College of Georgia suggests that adding progestin to ERT not only eliminates the risk but actually protects against breast cancer.

ENDOMETRIAL (UTERINE) CANCER

A number of studies first reported in 1975 found a small but significant risk of endometrial cancer in women treated postmenopausally with ERT. (Women who have had hysterectomies obviously have no risk of uterine cancer.) The rate increases from 4.5 to 13.9 times normal beginning after approximately two to four years' use of 0.625 or 1.25 milligrams of conjugated estrogen per day. Because endometrial cancer can often be successfully treated (for reasons that are still unclear—it may be that endometrial cancer is less virulent than other common cancers), reported death rates from endometrial cancer have not increased due to greater estrogen use. In fact persons with endometrial cancer do not have any higher reported mortality rate than the normal population.

Endometrial cancer was thought to be rare among women who use ERT only a few years or less. However, a study reported in

1985 by the Boston University School of Medicine found the risk of uterine cancer increased threefold in women who had taken conjugated estrogen for as little as a year or longer, and risks did not seem to decline even ten years after estrogen use stopped. The risk appears to increase with length of use, so that among those on ERT for five years or more, 11 percent are likely to develop endometrial cancer. All forms of estrogen not produced directly by the body, whether synthetic, natural, conjugated, or unconjugated, are considered potentially carcinogenic.

An endometrial aspiration biopsy is advised before ERT is prescribed, with repeated examinations every year to detect problems in early stages. The method of administering ERT may also affect the risk. Recent studies suggest that combining low doses of estrogen with progestin greatly reduces endometrial hyperplasia (a premalignant increase in cells in the lining of the uterus) and perhaps the risk of uterine cancer. The usual ERT regimen is the lowest effective dose of estrogen for three weeks, with progestin added the last ten days if the woman still has her uterus. Otherwise estrogen is given alone. Then drugs are discontinued for a week.

An unwelcome side effect with progestin for many women is that uterine bleeding, similar to a menstrual period, is triggered by the hormone-free days. Note that all uterine bleeding should be promptly investigated by evaluation of the endometrium, or lining of the uterus, since it may indicate serious problems other than the usual withdrawal bleeding from progestin use. Irregular spotting, fluid retention, and depression are other possible side effects. Most importantly, long-term effects of progestin use on postmenopausal women are unknown at present. For example, progestin suppresses blood levels of HDL; therefore it may have a potential for increasing atherosclerosis from long-term use. Since progestin has not been shown to be protective against any other estrogen side effect than endometrial hyperplasia, the danger is that other disorders may be produced in the attempt to avoid uterine cancer.

OVARIAN CANCER

There is contradictory evidence that ERT after menopause may increase the risk of ovarian cancer, though taking birth control pills earlier in life seems to reduce the risk.

EFFECTS ON EMOTIONS AND SLEEP

Psychological problems like anxiety and depression have not been shown to be directly relieved by ERT. Rather, improvements in emotional well-being, including better sleep, during estrogen use are thought to derive from the relief of physical symptoms.

SKIN AND HAIR CHANGES

Despite claims that it retards the aging process, there is no reliable evidence that estrogen prevents or reverses skin wrinkling, hair graying, or other signs of physical aging.

CURRENT GUIDELINES FOR ERT TREATMENT

Generally agreed-upon guidelines are now available for various estrogen deficiency states (see Table 3). If ERT is used, it is generally accepted that the lowest effective dose for the shortest possible period of time is desirable unless the purpose of therapy is the prevention or treatment of osteoporosis, requiring a larger dosage. Thus vasomotor symptoms like hot flashes are more readily treated than other symptoms, since they are usually short-lived phenomena. Previous typical menopausal dosages in the United States were 1.25 milligrams daily—2.5 milligrams daily in some countries. Current recommendations are for much lower dosages. Conjugated estrogens in the amount of 0.3 to 0.6 milligrams per day or ethinyl estradial in the amounts of 0.01 to 0.02 milligrams per day are given for the first twenty-one to twenty-five days of each menstrual cycle and then discontinued. ERT for hot flash symptoms can usually be discontinued altogether after a few years. The usual procedure is gradually to slow down until estrogen is stopped completely.

The local application of estrogen-containing creams in the vagina has become common in an attempt to avoid some of the systemic side effects of estrogen taken orally. However, these creams are rapidly absorbed into the bloodstream and the consequences of this absorption, especially in the endometrium, require further study. The biological effects of rapid entry into the blood without initial metabolism by the liver also needs examination. As a further complication, vaginal estrogen may be absorbed through the penis during sexual intercourse, causing enlargement and tenderness of the male breast tissue.

Table 3 Guidelines for the Use of Estrogens in Specific Deficiency States

---

I. The young woman (under 45 years of age) with both ovaries and uterus removed:
1. Choice of estrogen: A conjugated "natural" estrogen (see list of estrogen preparations, page 79).
The lowest effective dose should be used.* [Current medical opinion is shifting toward use of higher dosages (.625 mg minimum) for such women in order to prevent osteoporosis.—Authors]
2. Dosage schedule: Once daily from the 1st through the 25th day of each month.
NOTE: *If the uterus is present, it is advisable to add a progestin (medroxyprogesterone), 5 to 10 mg daily during the last 7 to 10 days of the estrogen course.†*
3. Duration of use: If well tolerated, until 50 years of age, when assessment of continued need is made individually.
4. Periodic examinations:
Baseline mammogram (low-radiation-dose xeroradiography); mammogram should be repeated only as necessary to evaluate possible breast tumor (American Cancer Society guideline).
Self-examination of breasts monthly.
Physician's examination of breasts (and uterus if present) every 6 to 12 months.

II. The woman experiencing the "menopausal syndrome" of hot flashes and sweating (usually 45 to 55 years of age):
A. Uterus not removed
1. Choice of hormones and recommended dosage range:
Estrogen: Conjugated equine estrogens—0.3 to 0.625 mg daily. (See list of alternative estrogen preparations, page 79.)
Progestin: Medroxyprogesterone—5 to 10 mg daily. The lowest effective dose of estrogen should be used.*
2. Dosage schedule:
Estrogen: Once daily from the 1st through the 25th day of each month.
Progestin: Once daily during the last 7 to 10 days of the estrogen course.†
3. Duration of use: 6 to 12 months, followed by gradual reduction of dose over a period of 2 to 3 months, and then discontinuation to assess the need for continued use. Treatment should be resumed only if symptoms require it. An attempt should be made to discontinue all hormones after 2 to 3 years of continuous use.

---

* The lowest effective dose is determined by keeping a daily "flash count" to ascertain the lowest daily dose that will reduce the frequency and severity of flashes to an acceptable level.
†The use of a supplemental progestin during the last 7 to 10 days of estrogen administration is still controversial. A possible benefit is the reduced potential for uterine cancer; a possible risk is the increased potential for coronary artery disease; a possible inconvenience is withdrawal bleeding (induced menstruation). The risks of this form of long-term progestin therapy are not known.

(Continued)

4. Periodic examinations:
   Baseline mammogram (low-radiation-dose xeroradiography).
   Low-dose mammogram annually (over 50 years of age) during continuous use of estrogen (American Cancer Society guideline).
   Self-examination of breasts monthly.
   Physician's examination of breasts every 6 to 12 months.
   Cervical cytology and endometrial biopsy (aspiration curettage) annually.
   Blood pressure measurement every 3 to 6 months.
   Two-hour blood sugar assay annually.

B. Uterus removed
   1. Choice of estrogen and dose: Conjugated equine estrogens—0.3 to 0.625 mg daily.
      The lowest effective dose should be used.*
   2. Dosage schedule: Once daily from the 1st through the 25th day of each month.
   3. Duration of use: 6 to 12 months, followed by gradual reduction of dose over a period of 2 to 3 months, and then discontinuation to assess the need for continued use. Treatment should be resumed only if symptoms require it. An attempt should be made to discontinue all hormones after 2 to 3 years of continuous use.
   4. Periodic examinations:
      Baseline mammogram (low-radiation-dose xeroradiography).
      Low-dose mammogram annually (over 50 years of age) during continuous use of estrogen (American Cancer Society guideline).
      Self-examination of breasts monthly.
      Physician's examination of breasts every 3 to 6 months.
      Blood pressure measurement every 3 to 6 months.
      Two-hour blood sugar assay annually.

III. The woman in the "postmenopausal" period (usually over 55 years of age): Treatment should be individualized as follows:
   1. If there are no specific symptoms of estrogen deficiency (hot flashes or atrophic vaginitis), estrogen should not be given.
   2. If specific symptoms of estrogen deficiency persist to a degree requiring subjective relief, the recommendations in category II apply. However, in addition to limiting courses of estrogen to 6 to 12 months followed by gradual withdrawal, dosage might be limited to 3 times weekly on a trial basis. Estrogen should be discontinued altogether as soon as possible. If only flashes persist beyond 60 years of age, all estrogen should be discontinued. Nonhormonal drugs such as clonidine, ergot preparations, and certain sedatives may be effective for the relief of hot flashes in some women.
   3. Although we do not yet have accurate and reliable predictive indicators, an attempt should be made to identify the woman who may be at high risk for the development of osteoporosis. The following features suggest the possibility of increased risk:
      (a) slender build, light-boned, Caucasian or Oriental race
      (b) a sedentary life-style, or restricted physical activity
      (c) a family history (mother or sister) of osteoporosis (reported by some investigators)
      (d) a low-sodium diet (also likely to be a low-calcium diet)

*The lowest effective dose is determined by keeping a daily "flash count" to ascertain the lowest daily dose that will reduce the frequency and severity of flashes to an acceptable level.

(e) heavy smoking
(f) excessive use of antacids that contain aluminum
(g) long-term use of cortisone-related drugs
(h) habitual use of carbonated beverages (reported by some investigators)
(i) excessive consumption of alcohol
(j) increased urinary excretion of calcium*

For the woman thought to be at increased risk for the development of osteoporosis, estrogen treatment should be started within 3 years after menstruation ceases. The following schedule of estrogen therapy may be recommended for prevention: conjugated equine estrogens—0.625 mg daily or 3 times weekly, for the first 3 weeks of each month. Periodic examinations as outlined in category II above should be performed. Estrogen replacement therapy may continue until 65 years of age,† always with appropriate supervision.

In addition to the prudent use of estrogen, regular exercise and a daily intake of 1500 mg of calcium‡ and 400 international units of vitamin D§ are generally thought to be beneficial in slowing the development of osteoporosis.

CONJUGATED ESTROGENS
The following conjugated estrogens are available for use in treating the menopausal syndrome. These are often called the "natural" estrogens, but they may be derived from natural or synthetic sources.

• Conjugated equine estrogens (Genisis, Premarin)
• Esterified estrogens (Evex, Menest)
• Estradiol cypionate (Depo-Estradiol Cypionate, injection)
• Estradiol valerate (Delestrogen, injection)
• Estriol (Hormonin, a mixture of estriol, estradiol, and estrone)
• Piperazine estrone sulfate (Ogen)
• Micronized 17B estradiol (Estrace)

Reprinted from The Essential Guide to Prescription Drugs, fourth edition, by James W. Long, M.D. (Harper & Row, 1985).

* Lactose intolerance and premature menopause (before age 45–50) are also recognized as additional risk factors.—Authors
†Age sixty-five is an arbitrary cutoff. Estrogen therapy can continue to any age unless contraindicated.—Authors
‡The dose generally found in a multiple-vitamin tablet.—Authors
§ About five glasses of milk (preferably skim) or its equivalent in calcium.—Authors

If estrogen is being given long-term for vaginal atrophy and/or the prevention of osteoporosis (the usual dosage for osteoporosis is .625 milligrams daily), the addition of progestin (for example in the form of Provera, 10 milligrams/day) from day sixteen through day twenty-five of the ERT cycle may help prevent endometrial cancer. However, as we discussed earlier, the long-term effects of progestin are unknown in older women.

Because of the established increased risk of developing endometrial cancer and gall bladder disease as well as possible risks such as hypertension, liver problems, and altered blood clotting, all women receiving ERT must have twice-yearly examinations for blood pressure elevation, breast masses, and the development of endometrial hyperplasia as well as endometrial cancer. An endometrial biopsy is recommended before ERT is begun and on a yearly basis thereafter, especially if a woman is receiving estrogen alone. A regular Pap smear should include material from the endocervical canal, since this enhances the otherwise unreliable detection of endometrial cancer. Regular blood tests for glucose, cholesterol, HDL, triglycerides, and liver function are also recommended.

The risks of estrogen may one day be ameliorated by the use of different varieties of estrogen, routes of administration, frequency, and dosages. Meanwhile the assessment of the pros and cons is necessarily part of weighing a decision whether to take estrogen. For example, the risk of dying from endometrial cancer is very low (see page 74), while possible, lifesaving benefits may be obtained from using estrogen to retard osteoporosis. Benefits may also outweigh risks if it can eventually be shown that estrogen protects against heart disease. On the other hand, the possible benefit of reduced potential for uterine cancer with estrogen-progestin combined may be overshadowed by the possible risk of increased potential for coronary artery disease or the inconvenience of monthly bleeding due to the added progestin.

OTHER FORMS OF SELF-CARE AND TREATMENT

Because of fears regarding estrogen, nonmedical treatments of menopause are receiving increasing attention. Adequate nutrition, exercise, education about symptom management, and group support are less drastic and often effective self-care methods. Since only about 25 percent of women go to their doctors with menopausal symptoms, 75 percent are handling menopause on their own.

Adequate nutrition is important in maintaining equilibrium during menopause. A good diet may be supplemented with vitamins C and D and calcium for bone health (see the section on osteoporosis in Chapter 9). Vitamin A may help heavy bleeding occurring around the time of menopause. Magnesium promotes relaxation and some women report that moderate amounts of vitamin E help leg cramps and modify hot flashes. Vitamin B complex may be useful in reducing edema and stress. However, brewer's yeast or other nutritional yeast can heighten vasomotor symptoms and may need to be avoided or reduced. Alcohol, caffeine, chocolate, white-flour products, tranquilizers, sleeping pills, and antidepressants all tend to aggravate menopausal symptoms, particularly hot flashes.

Relaxation techniques, meditation, massage, and yoga may reduce stress, fatigue, and depression. Acupuncture may be useful for conditions such as tension, lower back pain, and neckache. Aerobic exercise is generally useful in reducing menopausal fatigue, tension, and depression.

Nonmedical treatment for vaginal dryness and accompanying sexual discomfort is often helpful. Vaginal lubricants that are water-based (dissolve in water), such as K-Y jelly, Lubafax, Today, and Ortho Personal Lubricant, can be used to avoid or control vaginal dryness and irritation during intercourse. They cannot, however, reverse vaginal atrophy. Women should avoid oil-based lubricants such as petroleum jelly as well as lubricants like saliva because they may promote bacterial growth and lead to infection. Allowing more time for sexual stimulation and for the eventual appearance of natural vaginal lubrication is another simple and often effective technique.

The bacterial or viral cystitis that may become more frequent after menopause is often preventable or reversible. Careful washing of the woman's vaginal area and the man's penis with soap and water before sexual activity helps reduce potential infection. Urination before lovemaking is recommended since a full bladder is more easily irritated. Immediately after intercourse, it is helpful to drink large amounts of water and to urinate as soon as possible, thereby flushing out any disease agents. See Table 4 for an extensive list of preventive and self-treatment techniques for mild cystitis infection. If symptoms persist, medical care is necessary, including a urine analysis, a urine culture, medical treatment, and a later recheck of urine to make certain the cystitis is totally gone.

If douching is recommended by a physician for a vaginal infection, a homemade douche of two tablespoons of white vinegar mixed with two quarts of quite warm—not hot—water is effective. Fill a clean douche bag (or a hot-water bottle with a douching attachment) with the fluid, hang the container a foot or so above the floor of the bathtub, and lie down in the tub. Insert the nozzle about an inch and a half into the vagina and *slowly* release the clamp so the water runs in gently and drains back out. Baking soda (one tablespoon per quart of water) is sometimes recommended instead of vinegar; follow the doctor's recommendation. Commercially prepared douches are unnecessary and expensive. A number of them contain substances that can cause irritation or allergic reactions.

Table 4 Preventing Urinary Tract Infections, Treating Mild Infections, and Avoiding Reinfections

1. Drink lots of fluid every day. Try to drink a glass of water every two or three hours. (For active infection, drink enough to pour out a good stream of urine every hour. It really helps!)

2. Urinate frequently and try to empty your bladder completely each time. Never try to hold your urine once your bladder feels full.

3. Keep the bacteria in your bowels and anus away from your urethra by wiping yourself from front to back after urinating or having a bowel movement. Wash your genitals from front to back with plain water or very mild soap at least once a day.

4. Any sexual activity that irritates the urethra, puts pressure on the bladder or spreads bacteria from the anus to the vagina or urethra can contribute to cystitis. Make sure that you and your lover have clean hands and genitals before sex, and wash after contact with the anal area before touching the vagina or urethra. To prevent irritation to the urethra, try to avoid prolonged direct clitoral stimulation and pressure on the urethral area during oral-genital sex or masturbation. Make sure your vagina is well lubricated before intercourse. Rear-entry positions and prolonged vigorous intercourse tend to put additional stress on the urethra and bladder. Emptying your bladder before and immediately after sex is a good idea. If you tend to get cystitis after sex despite these precautions, you may want to ask your practitioner for preventive tablets (i.e., sulfa, ampicillin, nitrofurantoin); a single dose of a tablet after sex has been shown effective in preventing infections and is usually not associated with the same negative effects as prolonged courses of antibiotics.

5. Some birth control methods can contribute to or aggravate a urinary tract infection. Women taking oral contraceptives have a higher rate of cystitis than those not on the Pill. Some diaphragm users find that the rim pressing against the urethra can contribute to infection. (A different-size diaphragm or one with a different type of rim may solve this problem.) Contraceptive foams or vaginal suppositories may irritate the urethra. Dry condoms may put pressure on the urethra, or the dyes or lubricants may cause irritation.

6. If you use sanitary napkins during your period, the blood on the pad provides a convenient bridge for bacteria from your anus to travel to your urethra. Change pads frequently and wash your genitals twice a day when you are menstruating. Some women also find that tampons or sponges put pressure on the urethra.

7. Tight jeans, bicycling or horseback riding may cause trauma to the urethra. When you engage in sports that can provoke cystitis in you, wear loose clothing and try to drink extra water.

8. Caffeine and alcohol irritate the

bladder. If you don't want to stop using them, try to drink less of them and drink enough water to dilute them.

9. Some women find that routine use of cranberry juice (preferably the kind without sugar) or vitamin C to make their urine more acid helps to prevent urinary tract problems. (If you have an infection, try combining 500 milligrams of vitamin C and cranberry juice four times a day; you can substitute fresh cranberries in plain yogurt for the juice.) Whole grains, meats, nuts and many fruits also help to acidify the urine. Avoid strong spices (curry, cayenne, chili, black pepper).

10. Diets high in refined sugars and starches (white flour, white rice, pasta, etc.) may predispose some women to urinary tract infections.

11. Women use a wide variety of herbal remedies to prevent or treat urinary tract infections. Drinking teas made of uva ursi, horsetail or shavegrass, cornsilk, cleavers, comfrey, lemon balm or goldenseal may be beneficial to the bladder. You may want to consult a herbalist.

12. Keep up your resistance by eating and resting well and finding ways to reduce stress in your life as much as possible.

13. Vitamin B_6 and magnesium-calcium supplements help to relieve spasm of the urethra which can predispose you to cystitis. This is especially helpful for women who need to have their urethras dilated repeatedly.

14. If you have an infection, soak in a hot tub two or three times a day; try a hot water bottle or heating pad on your abdomen and back.

Reprinted from The New Our Bodies, Ourselves *by the Boston Women's Health Book Collective (Simon & Schuster, 1984).*

As a preventive measure, the wearing of cotton underwear rather than nonabsorbent nylon or other synthetics can help avoid infections by allowing air to circulate in the vaginal area. For the same reason, girdles, panty hose, and tight slacks should not be worn by women susceptible to infection.

Since the clitoral area of woman after menopause is often more senstive to trauma or irritation, sexual partners need to be thoughtful about touching this area in a way that does not produce pain. Women should be frank in telling their partners what is pleasurable and what is not. The discomfort of "honeymoon cystitis" caused by friction may be alleviated by changes in sexual positioning. The male partner should thrust his penis toward the back of the vagina and in the direction of the rectum, rather than toward the upper part of the vagina. This protects the bladder and the delicate urethra.

Although still controversial, there is some evidence that regular sexual activity helps preserve functioning, especially lubricatory ability, and may even stimulate estrogen production (remember that estrogen is produced in the adrenal glands and from body tissue in addition to the ovaries). Sexually active women also seem to have less vaginal atrophy, but it is unclear whether this is cause or effect. The regular muscle contractions during sexual activity and orgasm do maintain vaginal muscle tone and it is thought that intercourse helps preserve the shape and size of the vaginal space.

It is, of course, impossible for numbers of women to continue sexual contact after the illness or death of their partners. In addition, many women have never married or are divorced or separated. For those without partners, self-stimulation (masturbation) can be effective in preserving lubricating ability and the muscle tone that maintains the size and shape of the vagina. In addition, it can release tensions, stimulate sexual appetite, and contribute to general well-being. Self-stimulation is probably more common among younger women because they have grown up in a less restrictive sexual atmosphere. But it seems clear that self-stimulation is being practiced by women of all ages with increasing frequency, lessened anxiety, and considerable physical benefit.

Group support from women going through or having already completed menopause is especially helpful. Women are beginning to organize such groups just as younger women have organized around issues of pregnancy and childbirth. A menopause support group that serves as one of the first models is conducted by Dr. Fredi Kronenberg, Columbia College of Physicians and Surgeons, Box 348, 630 West 168th Street, New York, N.Y. 10032. We envision widespread use of "midwife equivalents" for the menopause—trained women who would be available as consultants to teach what to expect during menopause, evaluate symptoms, plan exercises, relaxation, diet, and home remedies, and organize support groups.

WHAT WE STILL NEED TO LEARN

There are now forty million women over forty, and thirty-one million of these are past menopause. All are subject to pre- and post-menopausal disorders, many of which can affect sexuality. The proportion of women over forty compared to the rest of the population will increase in the near future. Therefore, the understanding and treatment of menopausal disorders is and will become an even greater piece of the health care of mature women.

Participants in the National Institute on Aging's National Consensus Conference on Estrogen for postmenopausal women in 1979 listed a number of topics that require further study in order for women and their physicians to be able to make truly informed decisions regarding estrogen. These topics include:

- The natural course of menopause and the postmenopause.
- Social and cultural expectations regarding menopause.
- The cause(s) of hot flashes.
- The relationship of estrogen status to urinary tract symptoms.
- The effect of estrogen use on the risk of bone fractures.
- The effects of estrogen on psychological variables and on sleep.
- The relationship of risk of endometrial cancer to duration and recency of estrogen use.
- The value of various methods of early detection of endometrial cancer and endometrial hyperplasia.
- The relationship of estrogen use to risk of breast cancer.
- The relationship of estrogen use to risk of ovarian cancer.
- The relationship of estrogen use to gall bladder disease.
- Cardiovascular effects of estrogen use (including effects on serum lipid levels).
- Characteristics correlated with a high likelihood of benefiting from estrogen use.
- Characteristics correlated with a high risk of suffering undesirable effects of estrogens.
- Appropriateness of estrogen use by women undergoing premature menopause.
- Effects of various routes of estrogen administration, including placement of estrogen pellets under the skin and the use of locally applied estrogens in the vagina.
- The relationship of dose to various favorable and unfavorable effects of estrogens.
- Favorable and unfavorable effects of administering progestins along with estrogens.
- Investigation of alternative ways of preventing and managing menopausal conditions.

In the meantime, women need to be continuously informed about the changing state of knowledge so that they and their doctors can make decisions based on the latest evidence. Alternative methods other than estrogen use for preventing and treating sexual and other symptoms must be emphasized wherever feasible. But in the end, women and their doctors must make choices based on a presently incomplete understanding of risks and benefits—but an understanding that is growing and already makes some choices clearer.

7

THE SEXUAL EFFECTS OF SURGERY ON SEX ORGANS

It's not surprising that people are apprehensive about surgery on their sex organs. They dread possible sexual consequences in addition to the usual risks involved in any surgical procedure. Women commonly believe removal of the womb (hysterectomy) or of a breast (mastectomy) makes them "less of a woman." Men worry that prostate surgery means the end of sex life altogether. It is reassuring to know that the medical evidence does not support many of these fears, as long as surgeons are skilled, knowledgeable about the possible problems, and sensitive to patients' interest in preserving sexual functioning.

HYSTERECTOMY

A hysterectomy is the removal of the womb or uterus. In addition, the ovaries and Fallopian tubes may also be removed (bilateral salpingo-ovariectomy). It is estimated that 40 percent of American women over age forty and more than half of all women at age sixty-five will have had a hysterectomy, making this the most common major operation performed in the United States (nearly 700,000 hysterectomies in 1984). The U.S. has twice the rate of hysterectomies as England or Sweden. Evidence is growing that a proportion of these operations are unnecessary, especially those performed to sterilize a woman, to relieve symptoms of menstruation or menopause, or to attempt to prevent cancer of the ovaries and uterus. A second or third opinion about the need for surgery is strongly suggested. HERS (Hysterectomy Educational Resources and Services) offers counseling and support to women and their families faced with the question of surgery. Write 501 Woodbrooke Avenue, Philadelphia PA 19119.

Many hysterectomies are done because of the presence of benign (noncancerous) tumors called fibroids, which are not troublesome so long as they remain small, but may require surgery if they enlarge, cause bleeding, or involve other organs. Prolapse of the uterus ("fallen uterus"); cancer of the cervix, the endometrium (lining of the uterus), or related organs; and severe, uncontrollable infection or bleeding are other legitimate reasons for a hysterectomy.

It is often said there is no medical evidence that careful removal of the uterus causes impairment of sexual sensations. Yet some women greatly depend on sensations from the cervix and womb to achieve orgasm through deep penile penetration and must learn after hysterectomy, other methods of arousal, such as more focus on clitoral stimulation. The rhythmic contractions of the uterus during orgasm are of course gone as a result of a hysterectomy. During the surgical repair, surgeons are not always careful to avoid shortening the vagina, which can lead to problems with intercourse. Correct positioning of the wound repair in the back of the vagina is also important. If intercourse is resumed too early after hysterectomy, there can be pain due to incomplete healing in the vagina. Most physicians recommend waiting six to eight weeks before sexual activity is begun again.

Unless ovarian blood supply is interfered with as a result of surgery, the removal of a single ovary has no known effect on a woman's hormone balance. The remaining ovary will produce enough estrogen for body needs. If both ovaries are removed, loss of estrogen can produce changes in the lining of the vagina unless the woman receives estrogen replacement therapy (see Chapter 6). If the woman has not yet reached menopause, she will have physical changes similar to those of menopause, but they will occur all at once rather than following the more gradual pattern of a natural menopause. Removal of the ovaries after menopause generally produces far fewer direct symptoms, because the ovaries have already stopped functioning or show a substantial reduction in estrogen output. One of the most common and troublesome symptoms is vaginal dryness and thinning of the vaginal walls. We have discussed methods of handling this in Chapter 6. Urinary problems can develop related to hormone changes or to the surgery itself and may require medical attention.

Total loss of ovarian function results in loss of ovarian androgen as well. Androgen, known for its role in producing sexual desire, is not replaced when a woman is given estrogen replacement therapy. (However, some androgens continue to be produced in the adrenal glands.) Currently there is no agreement on safe replacement therapy for androgen, nor is it known which women might need it. (However, an important Canadian study reported in 1985 presents evidence that would favor the use of androgen.) Tests are under way on a slow-release androgen pellet that is inserted surgically under the skin in the hip and replaced every six months. Such local administration of the hormone is thought to avoid the masculinizing effects of androgen taken orally or intravenously.

Many surgeons and women themselves warn that a period of emotional instability commonly begins about the third or fourth day after a hysterectomy and lasts two to five or ten days, or longer. Depression, sleep disturbances, fatigue, listlessness, weight gain, loss of appetite, weeping, and irritability may occur—physical and/or emotional responses to the surgery. Rarely are they severe or long lasting enough to require psychotherapeutic care. Most women regain their equilibrium naturally, although many claim that it takes six months or longer to fully recover physically, especially if the ovaries have been removed. *Coping with Hysterectomy* by Suzanne Morgan (Dial Press, 1982) is a useful guide for dealing with the issues surrounding hysterectomy.

Removal of all or parts of a woman's childbearing apparatus, powerful symbols of womanhood, often does have significant psychological effects. If the woman sees the surgery as symbolic "castration," she needs to resolve this, either on her own or with outside help. She must understand that removal of the sexual organs need not eradicate sexuality, cause her to feel unattractive, or diminish her womanliness. Preoperative and postoperative counseling, ideally with her partner present, can do much to allay a woman's fears and misapprehensions. Group discussions with other women who have had hysterectomies can be especially helpful. Women's health centers or hospital social workers may be able to arrange this.

Hysterectomies can have positive effects on sexuality, particularly if they are done to relieve painful or debilitating conditions like infection, urinary incontinence, heavy bleeding, or endometriosis. A return to pain-free good health can be a potent aphrodisiac. A side effect for women in the childbearing years who have completed their families is the relief from anxiety about pregnancy. However, hysterectomy is not considered to be a sensible contraceptive alternative if there is no other strong indication for surgery.

MASTECTOMY

While most breast lumps (80–90 percent) are found to be benign upon biopsy, unfortunately the likelihood of breast cancer increases with age. Full or partial breast removal, or mastectomy, is performed when a lump in the breast is found to be malignant (cancerous).

In spite of current controversy over whether breast cancer begins in the breast or is a systemic disease beginning elsewhere, most physicians emphasize early detection of lumps as a major means of combating the disease. In addition to routine examination by your physician and the use of newer techniques to help him or her in diagnosis (for example, mammography by low-voltage X rays), you should undertake regular monthly self-examinations. We recommend *The Breast Cancer Digest: A Guide to Medical Care, Emotional Support, Educational Programs and Resources* (Office of Cancer Communications, National Cancer Institute, Bethesda, MD 20003, 1984). Recent results of a large study in Sweden on women between ages forty and seventy-four show that regular mammograms cut death rates from cancer by almost one third.

There are different kinds of mastectomy, ranging from removal of the lump(s) and some adjacent tissue only, to the removal of the entire breast, the surrounding lymph glands, and chest muscles. These operations have understandable psychological implications for many women, because they not only change the outward appearance of the body but visibly alter a specific symbol of sexuality. Periodic depression, with consequences for one's sex life, is common and expected during the first year or two after a mastectomy. Aesthetic reactions to breast removal can be more difficult than with a hysterectomy, which leaves no obvious signs beyond an abdominal scar.

Although there is no physiological change in sexual capacity after mastectomy, women may temporarily lose their sexual desire out of embarrassment, the inability to accept the loss of the breast, and fear that they have become less attractive to their sexual partners. They are afraid the absence of the breast will be noticeable in public. A properly fitting prosthetic bra can relieve worries about public appearance, but reactions to breast loss by women themselves and their partners are not always so easily resolved. One useful technique is for women to talk frankly with other women who have already experienced a breast loss. Some physicians and hospitals arrange for such volunteers to counsel with women prior to and following surgery. The Reach to Recovery program of the American Cancer Society, begun by Terese Lazar in 1952, is a rehabilitation program for women who have had breast surgery. (A helpful free booklet, "Reach to Recovery," is available from local units of the American Cancer Society.) The program is designed to help with physical, psychological, and cosmetic concerns, and utilizes a carefully selected and trained corps of volunteers who have adjusted successfully to their own surgery. Other forms of individual and group support can be immensely relieving as well.

Men, too, need a period of adjustment to work out their feelings about breast surgery in their partners. In some cities, Reach to Recovery uses male volunteers to help men adjust to their wives' mastectomies. In sturdy relationships, time and affection often take care of disturbed feelings following breast removal. Severe and prolonged emotional upset may require professional psychotherapy. Do not avoid seeking aid in such cases; the odds are that it will help greatly, whether the problem is with you or with your mate.

Specific recommendations that may speed the resumption of a normal sex life include:

- Involving the partner in all aspects of the discussions around a mastectomy.
- Having the partner see the wound as early as possible after surgery, so the process of adjustment can begin.
- Resuming sexual activity as soon as possible.
- Finding sexual positions that will be comfortable. For the first weeks and months, the patient's wound will be sensitive. A preferred sexual position is to have the partner on top, supporting his upper body with his arms. This leaves the woman in a relaxed position on her back, with no stress on her chest area.
- Deciding together whether the woman wants to wear a prosthesis (a padded bra) during sexual contact or whether the couple can be comfortable without it. Many couples eventually eliminate the need for the cover-up.
- Sharing feelings openly and supporting each other emotionally. Both partners are likely to have periods of depression and anxiety due to the fear of death that cancer brings and to reactions to the loss of a valued body part. Couples who can share such feelings may not need further counseling after the initial adjustment period.

Breast cancer treatment today is highly controversial. A few years ago most surgeons performed what is called the Halsted radical mastectomy, removing the entire breast, underlying muscles, and the nearby lymph nodes. This left a woman with a sunken chest wall and impaired mobility of the arm. When it was discovered that surgeons in countries such as Canada and England were removing much less breast tissue and getting nearly identical survival rates, American surgeons began changing their approach. Most now do the modified radical mastectomy, which removes less muscle and fewer lymph nodes. This operation is less disfiguring. The remaining question is whether mastectomies are any more effective than lumpectomies (removal of the lump) combined with radiation. Further evidence is needed, although figures from Canada and Europe would suggest that the simpler, less invasive procedure may have equivalent survival rates.

VAGINAL RECONSTRUCTION

Women who have had a number of children, difficult childbirths, or tears in the opening of the vagina at the time of childbirth may have an excessively enlarged vagina. Anterior and posterior plastic repair, a surgical procedure, may reconstruct the vagina effectively and make sex more pleasurable. This is a delicate operation and requires an especially skilled surgeon who is also sensitive to the woman's needs. A second medical opinion on the advisability of surgery is recommended.

PROSTATECTOMY

As men grow older, up to half of them experience significant enlargement of the prostate. This usually begins after age forty or fifty, and almost all men over fifty have some degree of enlargement. Fifty to 75 percent have noticeable symptoms and at least half eventually require surgery. By age eighty prostate problems are almost universal, although in a few cases the prostate gland atrophies with extreme age. No one knows yet why the prostate undergoes growth in the midlife after a period of dormancy following adolescence. There is evidence that black men develop prostate enlargement an average of five years earlier than white men. There also appear to be lower rates of enlargement among non-American Asian men compared to American Asian men. Diet may be a factor, especially large amounts of fat. Some physicians believe a zinc deficiency may be involved, but there is no solid evidence for this. Zinc taken in small doses will do no harm, but it is not a medically proved treatment or preventive for prostate problems. When the enlargement is noncancerous, as is usually the case, it is called benign prostatic hyperplasia (too many cells) or BPH. BPH starts very gradually and may exist for years with no symptoms. In fact, many men remain symptomless throughout their lives except for the enlargement. A reliable and readable book for men and their partners is *What Every Man Should Know About His Prostate* by Monroe Greenburger, M.D., and Mary-Ellen Siegel, M.S.W. (Walker and Company, 1983).

The size of the enlarged gland is less significant than the amount of obstruction it produces at the neck of the bladder. Since the prostate gland is so close to the bladder and urethra, enlargement can produce problems with urination. Men may find themselves with some or all of the following symptoms: An enlarged prostate may increase the need and urgency to urinate or to get up to void during the night. There may be a delay in starting the stream of urine, a slowness or weakness in the stream, or even a total inability to urinate. Occasionally, small amounts of blood are present in the urine and during ejaculation. (Bleeding should always be medically evaluated, since it could also be a symptom of cancer.) The dribbling of urine after urination is common, requiring the use of paper tissues for a few minutes to catch the drops of urine. Since enlargement of the gland may lead to retention and stagnation of urine, there can be bacterial infection. In severe and untreated cases, damage is done to the kidneys. Surgery is absolutely necessary when a urinary shutdown occurs.

The causes of noncancerous prostatic difficulties are unknown but may be connected to genetics, to changes in endocrine levels, and/or to the aging process itself. Previous theories about changes in hormone levels seem to have been recently disproved at Johns Hopkins Medical School and elsewhere. A curious aspect of BPH is that it has been found in aging men and aging dogs, but in no other species. There is no foundation to the folklore that prostate trouble is related to "excessive" sexual activity. Indeed, evidence suggests that an active and regular sex life preserves healthy prostate functioning, while a pattern of irregular ejaculations may lead to problems such as inflammation.

Cancer of the prostate, a much more serious disorder, occurs largely in men over sixty. The cause is still unknown. It does not appear that men with BPH have higher rates of prostate cancer than those without BPH. Most such cancers are not detected until men are in their seventies, and cancer of the prostate is the second leading cause of cancer deaths in men, killing 25,500 annually. The probability of developing prostate cancer in one's lifetime is about 9 percent for American men. However, if detected early, many cases can be successfully treated with surgery and radiation. The cancer is relatively slow-growing and may go through dormant periods. A physical exam at least once a year after age forty, including a digital (finger) rectal examination and a complete urinalysis, greatly enhances the chance of early detection.

A new technique using an ultrasound probe in the rectum to study the entire prostate has been developed in Japan. It is still under experimental study at the Preventive Medicine Institute–Strang Clinic in New York, and elsewhere.

Advances in the medical (probably hormonal) treatment of benign prostatic hypertrophy seem promising but are not yet of practical use. A new treatment using a laser is currently being tested. The YAG laser is an intense light beam that can be used under local anesthesia to destroy the excess prostate tissue in benign prostatic enlargement. The tissue is then voided with the urine. The advantage of the laser is that it avoids other surgical procedures, and allows the extra tissue to be painlessly eliminated. This is still experimental, however, and not yet available for the general public. Surgery remains the treatment of choice. Some doctors now recommend surgery at an earlier point in the course of symptoms to avoid unnecessary complications and dire emergencies; this decision is made by patient and doctor.

There are three types of prostate surgery, all requiring anesthesia:

Transurethral resection, or TUR, is the commonest, least traumatic and safest procedure because it requires no outside incision. A thin, hollow fiber-optic tube is inserted in the penis, an electric loop is maneuvered through the tube, and the gland is removed. One disadvantage of this technique is that the tissue sometimes grows back. TUR is recommended chiefly when the prostate is not too enlarged, and for men after seventy.

Suprapubic or *retropubic* surgery (named for the site of the incision, above or behind the pubic bone) is performed when the gland is very large. The tissue is removed through an incision made in the abdomen.

Perineal surgery is used by some surgeons for men with substantial prostate enlargement who are in poor physical condition. There is very little post-operative bleeding or pain with this procedure. An even more radical perineal procedure is used in the surgical treatment of cancer of the gland. These procedures can be performed with a high degree of safety even on a very elderly man. An incision is made in the perineum between the scrotum and the anus, and most or all of the prostate is removed. Whether surgery is more effective than radiotherapy for operable prostate cancer is questioned. Radiotherapy, however, results in impotence in only about 50 percent of men, compared to the nearly 100 percent impotence caused by perineal surgery.

Potency is rarely affected by the TUR and suprapubic procedures, and some men experience increased potency because their prostatic problems have been eliminated. It is generally agreed that 80 percent of men return to their presurgery sexual functioning. Ten percent have improved sexual functioning while 10 percent have some or even total loss of the ability to achieve an erection. The perineal approach—especially the radical procedure—has been the chief physical cause of impotence following prostatic surgery because critical nerves are cut. Perineal surgery also may affect the ability to urinate by causing strictures to form in the urethra. Dilation of the urethra is then required.

FREEZING TECHNIQUE

For prostate cancer, a freezing technique, rather than gland removal, is being tested by urologist Maurice Gonder at the State University of New York at Stony Brook. This cryosurgery, used more widely in Europe, destroys the tumor cells and stimulates the body to produce an immune response against the tumor.

NERVE-SPARING SURGERY

In 1982 a "nerve-sparing operation" (a modified radical retropubic prostectomy), designed to protect the nerve centers damaged by the usual cancer surgery, was developed at Johns Hopkins by Dr. Patrick Walsh. A number of clinics now offer such surgery, which preserves potency in 70–90 percent of men who have the operation. A film that demonstrates this new technique is distributed free to surgeons by Norwich Eaton Pharmaceuticals, Norwich, N.Y.

Prior to surgery, prostate problems usually do not interfere with sexual functioning unless pain is present. Some men may experience a slight decrease in the force of their ejaculation, but others may have benign prostate problems for years with no change in sexual functioning. After a prostatectomy, as we have noted, most men return to normal sexual activity. Healing time runs at least six weeks and most men wait four to six weeks before resuming sexual activity. The only change after most types of surgery is that in many cases semen is no longer ejaculated through the penis but instead is pushed backward into the bladder (retrograde ejaculation), where it is voided with the urine. This so-called dry ejaculation happens because a space has been left where the enlarged prostate had been, and fluid travels the path of least resistance to the bladder. Although men in this situation can no longer father children, the large majority have erections as before, with no diminishment of sexual pleasure. (However, if couples wish, sperm can be successfully extracted from the urine and deposited in the female partner's vagina for fertilization purposes.) Couples of childbearing age should not depend on retrograde ejaculation for birth control, since some seman may pass down through the penis. In addition, normal ejaculation may return following some regrowth of the prostate; in such instances, fertility may be restored. A certain amount of regrowth can occur without causing difficulties before surgery is again, if ever, necessary.

By far the greatest cause of impotence occurring with prostatectomies is *psychological*. Unfortunately, family doctors and urologists do not always give a man adequate information about what to expect after surgery, so that he falsely assumes sexual impairment. This assumption, with its consequent fear, is based on the tendency to associate the prostate gland with the penis, since men know the two are in physical proximity.

Beware of the many quack remedies that promise treatment without surgery. Various kinds of massage, foods, and other "cures," often at exorbitant prices, are offered to men seeking a quick cure for a sometimes serious condition. Avoid them and rely on your physician's advice.

ORCHIDECTOMY

This surgery, removal of the testes, may follow cancer of the prostate. The psychological impact of this castration can be devastating. Emotional preparation before and counseling following surgery are indispensable. The creation of artificial testes of plastic or tantalum may be advisable for cosmetic and emotional reasons. Impotence does not always follow removal of the testes; some men continue with normal erections.

COLOSTOMY AND ILEOSTOMY

When part of the bowel must be removed for lifesaving purposes, the anus is generally closed and an artificial opening in the abdomen created. The surgery may be in the colon (colostomy) or in the ileum (an ileostomy). Needless to say, the patient has many sensitive adjustments to make after such surgery. A bag attached to the opening fills with feces and must be emptied, although many colostomy patients develop enough bowel predictability to simply wear a gauze pad. There are possible embarrassing bowel sounds as well as odors. Much of this can be controlled adequately. Patients have to work their way through their own feelings, however, as well as their perception of other people's attitudes. The most complicated issue of all can be the working out of the sexual relationship with one's partner. Specialized information, and perhaps counseling, can help greatly.

Estimates are that it may take up to a year to make a full and relatively comfortable adjustment to an ostomy. The patient's primary physician as well as the surgeon is central in helping patients anticipate and circumvent or resolve problems. Although most people are grateful that their lives have been spared by ostomies, it is normal to experience difficulties in accepting the changes in one's body. Patients who had active sex lives prior to ostomies usually continue to have them afterward, but inevitably there is a complex adjustment process, and patients and their partners should not hesitate to seek help. Over a million people in the United States have had ostomies, and United Ostomy Clubs have been formed, which can offer a great deal of help. For information on the local chapter nearest you (there are more than 250 nationwide), contact the United Ostomy Association, 1111 Wilshire Boulevard, Los Angeles, CA 90017. "Sex, Courtship and the Single Ostomate" is a pamphlet available from the association.

RECTAL CANCER SURGERY

If a cancerous tumor is operable and is not in the lower two-thirds of the rectum, surgery can be done that not only permits normal bowel function but also allows normal sexual activity. However, if removal of the tumor requires removal of the rectum and anus, with a permanent colostomy, men may become totally impotent. The closeness of male genital organs to the lower rectum leaves essential nerve fibers vulnerable to damage from such surgery. Women, though, maintain capacity for sexual arousal and orgasm even after rectal surgery, since the essential nerves involved are farther removed from the surgical site.

In general, for both men and women, the emotionally charged aspects of surgery and its effects on sexuality can be relatively short-lived if people spell out their fears and if their misconceptions are cleared up. Unfortunately, they often do not get the opportunity to do this. Doctors do not always take the time to explain procedures and answer questions, though counseling before surgery is extremely helpful in preventing anxiety and clarifying misunderstandings. After the operation, continued advice and emotional support from medical personnel, family and friends, and special organizations are crucial to adjustment. Be sure to ask for help, and if you remain troubled, seek professional psychotherapy to work through more complicated feelings.

Even under the best of modern techniques, rates of recovery vary with the individual after surgery of any kind. Some people find their stamina or vitality reduced for some time, even though healing has been satisfactory. Surgeons do not always make it clear to their patients that these are normal variations. You have no reason to worry if this happens to you, as long as your surgeon has assured you that your postoperative recovery is progressing as it should be. Once you are feeling entirely well again, your level of sexual activity is likely to return to normal.

8

THE EFFECTS OF MEDICATIONS AND ALCOHOL ON SEX

Drugs, prescription or otherwise, can and do cause serious sexual problems for both men and women. The impact on sexuality may range from major to subtle effects. Doctors often fail to consider the sexual consequences of drugs they prescribe; and patients are often unaware that the medications they are taking may influence sexual desire or functioning.

Consider your drug use if you are having sexual problems. A study reported in 1983 in the *Journal of the American Medical Association* found that 25 percent of sexual problems in men were either caused or complicated by medications. Less is known about the effects of drugs on female sexuality—but the assumption is that drugs affecting men will affect women as well. Some drugs interfere with the autonomic nervous system, which is involved in normal sexual response. Others affect mood and alertness or change the production or action of sex hormones. (See Tables 5 and 6.)

Table 5   Possible Drug Effects on Female Sexuality

Increased libido: androgens; chlordiazepoxide (*Librium*) (anti-anxiety effect); diazepam (*Valium*) (anti-anxiety effect); mazindol (*Sanorex*).

Decreased libido: (See list of drug effects on male sexuality. Some of these *may* have potential for reducing libido in the female. The literature is sparse on this subject.)

Impaired arousal and orgasm: anticholinergics; clonidine (*Catapres*); methyldopa (*Aldomet*); mono-amine oxidase inhibitors (MAOIs); tricyclic antidepressants (TADs).

Breast enlargement: penicillamine; tricyclic antidepressants (TADs).

Galactorrhea (spontaneous flow of milk): amphetamine; chlorpromazine (*Thorazine*); cimetidine (*Tagamet*); haloperidol (*Haldol*); heroin; methyldopa (*Aldomet*); metoclopramide (*Reglan*); phenothiazines; reserpine (*Serpasil, Ser-Ap-Es*); sulpiride (*Equilid*); tricyclic antidepressants (TADs).

Virilization (acne, hirsutism, lowering of voice, enlargement of clitoris): anabolic drugs; androgens; haloperidol (*Haldol*).

Table 6   Possible Drug Effects on Male Sexuality

Increased libido: androgens (replacement therapy in deficiency states); baclofen (*Lioresal*); chlordiazepoxide (*Librium*) (anti-anxiety effect); diazepam (*Valium*) (anti-anxiety effect); haloperidol (*Haldol*); levodopa (*Larodopa, Sinemet*) (may be an indirect effect due to improved sense of well-being).

Decreased libido: antihistamines; barbiturates; chlordiazepoxide (*Librium*) (sedative effect); chlorpromazine (*Thorazine*)10–20% of users; cimetidine (*Tagamet*); clofibrate (*Atromid-S*); clonidine (*Catapres*) 10–20% of users; diazepam (*Valium*) (sedative effect); disulfiram (*Antabuse*); estrogens (therapy for prostatic cancer); fenfluramine (*Pondimin*); heroin; licorice; medroxyprogesterone (*Provera*); methyldopa (*Aldomet*) 10–15% of users; perhexilene (*Pexid*); prazosin (*Minipress*) 15% of users; propranolol (*Inderal*) rarely; reserpine (*Serpasil, Ser-Ap-Es*); spironolactone (*Aldactone*); tricyclic antidepressants (TADs).

Impaired erection (Impotence): anticholinergics; antihistamines; baclofen (*Lioresal*); barbiturates (when abused); chlordiazepoxide (*Librium*) (in high dosage); chlorpromazine (*Thorazine*); cimetidine (*Tagamet*); clofibrate (*Atromid-S*); clonidine (*Catapres*) 10–20% of users; cocaine; diazepam (*Valium*) (in high dosage); digitalis and its glycosides; disopyramide (*Norpace*); disulfiram (*Antabuse*) (uncertain); estrogens (therapy for prostatic cancer); ethacrynic acid (*Edecrin*) 5% of users; ethionamide (*Trecator-SC*); fenfluramine ((*Pondimin*); furosemide (*Lasix*) 5% of users; guanethidine (*Ismelin*); haloperidol (*Haldol*) 10–20% of users; heroin; hydroxyprogresterone (therapy for prostatic cancer); licorice; lithium (*Lithonate*); marijuana; mesoridazine (*Serentil*); methantheline (*Banthine*); methyldopa (*Aldomet*) 10–15% of users; mono-amine

(Continued)

oxidase inhibitors (MAOIs) 10–15% of users; perhexilene (Pexid); prazosin (Minipress) infrequently; propranolol (Inderal) infrequently; reserpine (Serpasil, Ser-Ap-Es); spironolactone (Aldactone); thiazide diuretics 5% of users; thioridazine (Mellaril); tricyclic antidepressants (TADs).

Impaired ejaculation: anticholinergics; barbiturates (when abused); chlorpromazine (Thorazine); clonidine (Catapres); estrogens (therapy for prostatic cancer); guanethidine (Ismelin); heroin; mesoridazine (Serentil); methyldopa (Aldomet); mono-amine oxidase inhibitors (MAOIs); phenoxybenzamine (Dibenzyline); phentolamine (Regitine); reserpine (Serpasil, Ser-Ap-Es); thiazide diuretics; thioridazine (Mellaril); tricyclic antidepressants (TADs).

Decreased plasma testosterone: adrenocorticotropic hormone (ACTH); barbiturates; digoxin (Lanoxin); haloperidol (Haldol) (increased testosterone with low dosage, decreased testosterone with high dosage); lithium (Lithonate); marijuana;

medroxyprogesterone (Provera); mono-amine oxidase inhibitors (MAOIs); spironolactone (Aldactone).

Impaired spermatogenesis (reduced fertility): adrenocorticosteroids (prednisone, etc.); androgens (moderate to high dosage, extended use); antimalarials; aspirin (abusive, chronic use); chlorambucil (Leukeran); cimetidine (Tagamet); colchicine; co-trimoxazole (Bactrim, Septra); cyclophosphamide (Cytoxan); estrogens (therapy for prostatic cancer); marijuana; medroxyprogesterone (Provera); methotrexate; mono-amine oxidase inhibitors (MAOIs); niridazole (Ambilhar); nitrofurantoin (Furadantin); spironolactone (Aldactone); sulfasalazine (Azulfidine); testosterone (moderate to high dosage, extended use); vitamin C (in doses of 1 gram or more).

Testicular disorders: Swelling: tricyclic antidepressants (TADs). **Inflammation:** oxyphenbutazone (Tandearil). **Atrophy:** androgens (moderate to high dosage, extended use); chlorpromazine (Thorazine);

spironolactone (Aldactone).

Penile disorders: Priapism: cocaine; heparin; phenothiazines; **Peyronie's disease:** metoprolol (Lopressor).

Gynecomastia (excessive development of the male breast): androgens (partial conversion to estrogen); BCNU; busulfan (Myleran); chlormadinone; chlorpromazine (Thorazine); chlortetracycline (Aureomycin); cimetidine (Tagamet); clonidine (Catapres) infrequently; diethylstilbestrol (DES); digitalis and its glycosides; estrogens (therapy for prostatic cancer); ethionamide (Trecator-SC); griseofulvin (Fulvicin, etc.); haloperidol (Haldol); heroin; isoniazid (INH, Nydrazid); marijuana; methyldopa (Aldomet); phenelzine (Nardil); reserpine (Serpasil, Ser-Ap-Es); spironolactone (Aldactone); thioridazine (Mellaril); tricyclic antidepressants (TADs); vincristine (Oncovin).

Feminization (loss of libido, impotence, gynecomastia, testicular atrophy): conjugated estrogens (Premarin, etc.).

Tables 5 and 6 reprinted from "Many Common Medications Can Affect Sexual Expression" by James W. Long, M.D., Generations VI (1981).

PRESCRIPTION DRUGS

Tranquilizers, antidepressants, and certain antihypertensive agents (for controlling high blood pressure) have all been implicated in impaired erection in men. Effects on women are less well understood.

TRANQUILIZERS

Strong tranquilizers such as Mellaril (thioridazine) and other phenothiazines may cause failure to obtain an erection or to ejaculate even when the capacity for erection remains. Any tranquilizing drug, even a mild one such as Librium (chlordiazepoxide), can also act as a depressant on the sexual feelings of both women and men.

ANTIDEPRESSANTS

Antidepressants such as imipramine hydrochloride (Tofranil) also inhibit sexual desire. According to two reports in the February 1985 *Journal of Clinical Psychopharmacology*, adverse sexual side effects have been reported with all standard antidepressants. Such side effects are much rarer with a new drug, bupropion (Wellbutrin). This drug, released for sale in January 1986, may become an option for patients who require drugs for long-term depression and who suffer sexual side effects from tricyclic and other antidepressants. A cholinergic drug, bethanechol (Urecholine), has also been found useful in treating antidepressant-induced sexual dysfunction.

ANTIHYPERTENSIVES

Antihypertensive medications are the most common cause of impaired erection. "Blocking agents," one class of antihypertensive drugs, include methyldopa (Aldomet), which reduces the flow of blood into the pelvic area and so inhibits erection of the penis. Another drug used against hypertension, guanethidine (Ismelin), may inhibit ejaculation by blocking the nerves involved. Up to two thirds of men taking the medication have reported problems. Guanethidine also can cause retrograde ejaculation (see page 97).

The common antihypertensive reserpine can decrease sexual interest or, at times, induce impotence. Even the diuretics given for high blood pressure can cause problems.

Patients who develop sexual problems after taking antihypertensive medications may be tempted to discontinue or decrease medication without telling their doctor. This can be very dangerous, since the medication could be preventing a stroke. Remember that your doctor may be able to help without putting your life in danger. Some alternatives are to switch antihypertensives to use only a diuretic, and/or reduce dosages when feasible. Many physicians no longer prescribe medications for mild to moderate hypertension until patients have first tried to bring blood pressure under control by lowering salt intake, and by exercise and weight reduction. When drugs are necessary, one study suggests that one of the most effective regimens, with the least likelihood of sexual impairment, is a combination of an oral diuretic, hydralazine, and propranolol. However, propranolol, promoted at first for its lack of sexual side effects, has now been implicated as affecting sexuality, especially when higher dosages are used.

OTHER DRUGS

The corticosteroids taken for arthritis may produce at least temporary impotence. Analgesics (pain medications) may reduce sensitivity and therefore affect male sexual capacity. Aspirin taken over long periods of time for pain may reduce fertility. Cimetidine (Tagamet), used in the treatment of duodenal ulcers and one of the most widely sold medicines in the U.S., can cause impotence. Ranitidine (Zantac) is a possible substitute for cimetidine.

ALCOHOL

Most people do not realize that alcohol is a drug. Pharmacologically it is a depressant rather than a stimulant, though in small amounts it may relax sexual inhibition in a pleasant manner. In larger amounts, however, it usually interferes with sexual performance, reducing potency in males and orgasmic ability in females. At the very least, alcohol often produces drowsiness, which then interferes with sex. The excessive use of alcohol is a frequent and too little recognized factor in sexual problems, and often those who abuse alcohol fail to realize how much they are actually drinking.

One man of forty-eight gave a history that strongly suggested the involvement of alcohol in his sexual problems:

"I have been a heavy drinker all my life, but I do not consider myself to be an alcoholic. I enjoy every bit of my life except my sexual relationship with my wife. I have the urge but not the erection, making it impossible for normal intercourse."

Even a few drinks before sex can affect a man's sexual performance, especially as men reach their forties. Erections may be less firm and ejaculation more difficult. But though this effect is temporary and reversible in terms of physical capacity, it can frighten a man into believing he is impotent, and fear itself may prolong the impotence.

Up to 80 percent of men who drink heavily are believed to have serious sexual side effects, including impotence, sterility, or loss of sexual desire. Many of the effects of moderate to heavy drinking may be reversible if drinking stops in time. However, heavy drinking over a long period irreversibly destroys testicular cells, leaving men with shrunken testicles. Both sexual drive and sexual capacity can be damaged. Hormone production is often affected, resulting in a decrease in testosterone and a drop in the sperm count. Total sterility as well as impotence result. Chronic heavy drinking can also produce liver and brain damage that leads to excess production of female hormones and a feminized body appearance.

Women are affected by alcohol in many of the same ways as men. More than one drink before a sexual encounter can interfere with the ability to reach orgasm. Chronic heavy use of alcohol can damage the ovaries, causing menstrual and ovulatory abnormalities and a decrease in estrogen production. This in turn may lead to early menopause and signs of premature aging. Atrophy of the breasts, uterus, and vaginal walls and lessened lubrication in the vagina are common.

Tolerance for alcohol decreases with age (one cause is changing kidney excretory power), so that smaller and smaller amounts may begin to produce negative effects. It is wise to avoid drinking altogether for several hours before a sexual encounter, or at least to limit alcohol to one drink. Persons who choose to drink regularly should limit themselves to a maximum of one and a half ounces of hard liquor, one six-ounce glass of wine, or two-eight ounce glasses of beer in any twenty-four-hour period. Remember, too, that alcohol is very dangerous in combination with narcotic and non-narcotic drugs such as sleeping pills, sedatives, painkillers, antihistamines, antidepressants, and tranquilizers, because it can pyramid their effects. If you are taking drugs, do not drink without discussing it with your doctor.

TOBACCO

Because of its nicotine content, tobacco is also a drug, although not usually categorized as one. It may be a factor in impotence. There is an old German saying about male erectile capacity: *"Rauchen macht schlump"*—"Smoking makes [it] dangle." Toxic changes in the blood from nicotine may affect sex hormones. There is some evidence that men who smoke have lower levels of testosterone. Nicotine also constricts blood vessels, in some cases enough to affect blood flow to the penis. Long-term smokers with atherosclerosis or peripheral vascular disease can become impotent.

NARCOTICS AND OTHER DRUGS

Regular users of opiates like morphine and heroin are often sexually impaired. Males who are addicted are usually impotent.

Cocaine use is growing, as cocaine has become more readily available at lower prices. A primary attraction of cocaine is that initially it heightens sexual sensation in both men and women as a result of euphoria, increased energy, and self-confidence. With habitual use, however, individuals experience a lowered sense of self-esteem, together with insomnia, fatigue, anxiety, and depression, and even paranoia, hallucinations, and seizures. Women become nonorgasmic and men impotent. A national telephone aid line—800-COCAINE—has been established for those who want help in stopping cocaine use.

Marijuana can lead to decreased sexual interest and impotence as well as drying of the mucous membranes in the sex organs. Amphetamines can produce impotence, delayed or no ejaculation in men, and inhibition of orgasms in women. Regular users of such barbiturates as sedatives and hypnotics (sleeping pills) may become impotent.

A rare but exceedingly destructive condition called priapism can occur in men who use certain drugs such as butyl (or isobutyl) nitrate, known also as "poppers," to stimulate more frequent and longer-lasting erections. An antidepressant drug, trazodone (Desyrel) can also cause similar problems. Priapism is a persistent and often painful erection of the penis caused by blood becoming trapped in the corpora cavernosa—the chambers in the penis that fill with blood to create erections. The erection does not subside and emergency medical care is needed within twenty-four hours or less to avoid permanent damage to the penis and almost certain permanent impotence. Partial priapism—any unusual period of persistent erection which eventually goes away by itself—is a sign that something is wrong and medical advice and treatment are indicated.

AVOIDING PROBLEMS

Health care professionals who prescribe or monitor the use of drugs should be thoroughly familiar with each drug's potential for adverse effects on sexuality. (Dr. James W. Long's book *The Essential Guide to Prescription Drugs* [Harper & Row, 1987] is a useful reference.) It is also important to obtain a patient's sexual history before giving any drug that may affect sexuality. This allows comparisons to be made before and after drugs are taken. Patient drug usage should be reviewed regularly, including prescription and over-the-counter drugs, alcohol, and tobacco.

Doctors should carefully explain the potential sexual side effects of drugs.

Most drug-caused sexual impairment is reversible if the responsible drug is reduced, removed, or replaced by another. (Impairment due to chronic alcoholism and possibly marijuana use may *not* be reversible.) In cases of serious illness, obviously, sexuality may have to be partially or even totally sacrificed for a period of time in order to obtain the beneficial effects of drugs that are essential to treatment. But in many cases, alternative drugs, lower dosages, or other treatment altogether can be given. For example, an antihypertensive drug that may adversely affect one person's sexuality will not affect another's. The possible sexual side effects of a drug must be balanced against the risks of a disease, with the patient's preference a crucial factor in the decision.

9

TIPS FOR LIFELONG SEXUAL FITNESS

The enjoyment of sex is enhanced by a healthy, pain-free body. The overall formula for keeping in good health and preventing a multitude of problems after forty is a simple one: No smoking, moderate use of alcohol, control of blood pressure and weight, balanced nutrition, regular exercise, and adequate rest. Numerous studies are confirming what Aristotle knew and what we are constantly rediscovering with the sense of stumbling onto something new: Moderation and balance must be practiced in everything that has to do with the body. It's encouraging to read that a 1985 Gallup poll found that only 35 percent of adult Americans smoked, a decline from the high of 43 percent in 1972.

THE YEARLY PHYSICAL EXAM

Apart from visits to the doctor for a specific complaint, men and women should have a physical examination every year after forty. Women should have a gynecological examination every six months.

Any problems in sexual functioning should be brought to the doctor's attention at the time of these examinations, if not at a special appointment in between. (Your physician may need to be encouraged or even prodded by you to discuss sexual issues—see Chapter 13.) The purpose of all this is to detect and treat physical problems in their early stages and to provide the medical basis for a program of preventive health care, including exercise, nutrition, and rest.

EXERCISE

An exercise program can improve physical appearance, enhance your sex life, and even increase longevity. It helps preserve the functioning of the heart, arteries, and respiratory system and has a relaxing effect on the nervous system. Studies indicate that bones stay bigger and stronger if one exercises regularly. Exercise is credited with bringing about favorable emotional changes. The only bad news, as everyone knows, is that it requires discipline and a certain amount of work. Exercise should be planned on a routine and daily basis. If you decide to undertake exercise, you simply make time for it. Although we are improving our habits as a nation, many Americans still do not exercise wisely or regularly, and older people exercise less than younger people. This is unfortunate, since the older you are, the more help your body needs from you.

Physical fitness is a quality of life, a condition of looking and feeling good and having the necessary physical reserves to enjoy a range of interests, among which is sex. Fitness has two components. Basic health, or *organic fitness*, means a well-nourished body as free as possible from disease or infirmity. If there are physical limitations, they will have been compensated for to the greatest degree possible. The second component, *dynamic fitness*, refers to a person's being not simply free from disease but fully fit to move vigorously and energetically. This involves efficiency of heart and lungs, muscular strength and endurance, balance, flexibility, coordination, and agility.

Two distinct kinds of exercise are necessary: one to keep the body limber and supple and to strengthen the muscles (stretching and flexing exercises); the other to increase endurance and enlarge the heart capacity (aerobic exercises). To achieve fitness one should exercise aerobically at least twenty to thirty minutes three to five times a week, at about 70 percent of one's age-adjusted maximum heart rate. To find the maximum rate, subtract your age from 220. For example, a forty-five-year-old would subtract 45 from 220, which is 175. Seventy percent of 175 would equal 122 heartbeats per minute, or twenty beats every ten seconds. For aerobic benefit, fast walking, swimming, cycling, cross-country skiing, and skating, which involve continual movement, are preferred over basketball, dance, handball, tennis, and racquetball, which are intermittent in movement. Jogging and fast action sports like racquetball have an additional problem: They frequently cause injury to the bones and joints. If you have not been exercising, take four to six weeks to get slowly into shape. Warm up for five minutes with stretching exercises before more vigorous work, and cool down for five minutes afterward.

A recent explosion of books give guidance to the young and middle-aged on exercise. Interestingly, a growing number of exercise books are written specifically for older people, including those who are wheelchair-bound or bedridden. A good overall book for the middle and later years is *Fitness After Forty: An Exercise Prescription for Lifelong Health*, by Herbert DeVries and Dianne Hales (Scribner's, 1982), although there are many others.

After age forty, you would do well to discuss your health status and exercise plans with your doctor. Increasingly, well-qualified fitness advisors are available to help plan and implement an individualized fitness program. There are wide variations in physical performances and capacities. Your individual physical condition should determine your appropriate exercises, and their level and pace. If you become temporarily ill or inactive, you usually need to return to an earlier level of activity and slowly work your way back. In all cases, avoid strenuous bursts of sudden activity when you are out of shape. If you have been under severe work or personal stress and pressure, a week or two at a reputable health spa, though expensive, can be a valuable way to reorient your habits.

Brisk walking for at least an hour a day, accompanied by a regimen of calisthenics, is probably the best all-round exercise for midlife and especially for older people. The squeezing action of the leg muscles on the veins during walking helps promote the return of blood to the heart. Start by walking rapidly until you begin to feel tired. Rest and walk back to your starting point. Keep doing this, for longer distances, until you reach a reasonable goal (which may take a year or so if you have previously been idle), such as a fast walk of two to three miles a day in forty-five minutes or less.

If you have been unusually inactive or there has ever been indication of possible heart disease, jogging, swimming, and other more vigorous activities should be preceded by a treadmill stress test (available in most hospitals). Swimming is particularly useful for anyone with a joint disease like arthritis or orthopedic problems such as damaged knees or chronic backache. It is not recommended as the major physical activity to protect against osteoporosis, however, precisely because it is not weight-bearing on the long bones of the body. A bicycle machine has the advantages of being available in all kinds of weather, requiring no transportation to and fro (if you have one in your home), and allowing accurate measurement of how much exercise you are getting. However, one must have good knees and no major orthopedic problems. As a supplement to a regular program of exercise, you should take advantage of any opportunity for physical movement—walking upstairs, doing chores, mowing the lawn, gardening, dancing: in short, bending, stretching, and moving as much as possible.

Spa fitness centers and resorts have begun to pay more attention to the medical as well as the aesthetic and social aspects of exercise. Some of the best of these centers are a legitimate part of the health self-care movement that is growing in the United States. The same can be said of the best of the aerobic centers and health clubs that are proliferating in most cities. Most are coed and men must be warned that they will not usually be able to achieve the same level of flexibility as most women. This is not a sign that they are not trying hard enough. It simply means that male and female bodies are different and women are by nature more flexible. On the other hand, men often have a natural advantage over women in exercises that emphasize strength. Ideally, both men and women should approach exercise noncompetitively, focusing instead on individual capacity and self-improvement.

Some people don't exercise for fear that it will provoke a heart attack. But exercise opposes the effect of stroke or heart attack. Blood clots form when the blood is sluggish rather than when it is vigorous. A recent study of seventeen thousand middle-aged and older Harvard alumni over several years by Dr. Ralph Paffenburger and colleagues found a 49 percent excess risk of coronary heart disease among people who led sedentary life-styles. As described in Chapter 3, people who have had heart attacks are usually placed on an exercise program by their physicians shortly after initial recovery in order to reduce the possibility of another attack. Exercise is also valuable for preventing and treating hypertension, diabetes, and osteoporosis.

EXERCISING YOUR TROUBLE SPOTS

There are specific exercises that can greatly improve your appearance if you have got out of shape.

A protruding abdomen, the bane of multitudes of men and some women past forty, cannot be overcome by diet alone. Exercise is essential. One method is to lie flat on your back on the floor, knees bent, arms crossed over your chest, and to raise slowly your head and shoulders about halfway to a sitting-up position. Hold this position for a few seconds, gradually working up to a count of ten. Do this up to ten times a day. You should feel your stomach muscles tighten as you lift head and shoulders off the floor.

Improving back muscles also helps your stomach muscles, as well as preventing or alleviating back pain. As much as 80 percent of backaches are due to muscle fatigue rather than slipped disks or arthritis. Lie on your back, squeeze your buttocks together, and tighten stomach muscles, while flattening your back against the floor. Hold for a count of five, then relax; repeat ten times. Swimming is also an excellent conditioner for those with back problems.

If you feel any undue stress or pain, talk to your doctor to work out a safe program. Some people consult "exercise physiologists," a new specialty with training of its own, to work at individualized exercise programs. Get a referral from your physician or from a licensed physical therapist.

In what may be the female version of the potbelly, many women develop weakened pelvic muscles, which makes them feel the vagina is losing its gripping ability. If uncorrected, such muscular weakness can cause problems in support for pelvic organs, like the uterus and the bladder. The Kegel exercises for women consist of twenty to thirty contractions of the pubococcygeal muscles of the pelvic floor, as though one were holding oneself back from urinating and defecating at the same time. It should be possible to feel the muscles tightening. These exercises should be performed several times daily and can be done while one is in a sitting or standing position and otherwise occupied. Contractions are held only a few seconds, and the process must be repeated daily for a total of at least one hundred contractions for the Kegel exercises to be truly effective. In two to three months, muscle tone and control will improve. Sexual sensation may also improve, since the pubo-coccygeal muscle contains the nerve endings that provide pleasurable sensations in the outer third of the vagina. The exercise strengthens back muscles too.

When there is improved muscle tone as a result of using Kegel exercises, the vaginal walls exert greater pressure on the penis during intercourse. This is of particular value in older couples when the man's penis has become somewhat smaller and the woman's vagina larger. Some women are able to use the Kegel movement in a rhythmic fashion during sexual intercourse, increasing the satisfaction to both partners. The exercises also help to support the pelvic structure—the uterus, bladder, and rectum. Some physicians prescribe Kegel exercises to treat or prevent prostatitis in men.

NUTRITION

Habitual poor nutrition begins to catch up with people as they reach midlife. There is an illusion, shared even by medical professionals, that the United States is the world's best-fed nation. This is not true. Millions of babies and their mothers are ill-nourished. Many teenagers live on fast foods. Most middle-aged persons consume too much fat, salt, sugar, and alcohol. In old age, frequent poverty or near-poverty can limit the amount of money available for food, especially good quality food. Social isolation and depression can cause older people to lose their appetites and stop taking an interest in cooking; physical limitations may make shopping and preparing foods difficult; loss of teeth or poor teeth interfere with eating solid foods; illnesses and chronic diseases of many kinds can affect food consumption; and finally, poor eating habits may develop in later life (snacking, the tea-and-toast syndrome, junk and convenience foods like TV dinners). People of any age who live alone are especially prone to neglect proper diets—"It's too much bother to fix a meal for just one person."

What are the dangers of poor nutrition? Vulnerability to disease, fatigue, loss of a sense of well-being, greater likelihood of emotional problems—among them depression, apathy, anxiety—all these are possible effects of inadequate diet. Further, age-related processes can be accelerated, and sexual interest and performance are often lowered. Thus there are a great many reasons to eat well, aside from the pleasure of good food itself.

Ideally, food habits should be reviewed periodically. Because people usually eat fewer calories as they grow older, the quality of those calories must improve; a comprehensive picture of one's diet should include a chart of food intake for twenty-four hours, a food preference record, and a chronological history of one's dietary habits.

A healthy diet includes three kinds of foods—proteins (meat, dairy products, eggs, fish, poultry, beans, nuts, and some grains), carbohydrates (cereals, breads, vegetables, fruits), and fats (meat, dairy products, oils, nuts, and grains). Carbohydrates, the complex starches and natural sugars appearing in fruits, vegetables, and grains, are emerging as the overall healthiest foods, supplemented by poultry, fish, and low-fat dairy products. Red meat, any kind of animal or dairy fat, and egg yolks should be strictly limited. Refined carbohydrates, both sugars and starches, are often the cheapest foods, and both people with a sweet tooth, who love sugar, and those on a low budget, who find starchy foods filling, may overload their diets with them. Refined starches, sugar, and other sweeteners fill the stomach, raise the blood sugar, lower the appetite, and lead to a false sense of well-being. Do not be deceived. You must have a much more balanced diet every day for vitality and body-tissue repair.

If you happen to be overweight and need to diet, a good general reference is *Jane Brody's Nutrition Book* (W. W. Norton, 1981), as well as *Jane Brody's Good Food Book* (W. W. Norton, 1985). Avoid crash and fad diets, since they can harm your health and your appearance. Develop food habits you can live with comfortably in good health while still losing weight. Diet clubs such as TOPS, Weight Watchers, Overeaters Anonymous, or informally organized weight-loss support groups (you can organize your own) can assist people with persistent weight problems.

Sexual activity expends calories but not enough for it to qualify as a form of weight reduction. In the most active period before and after orgasm, one uses only about 6.4 calories per minute, with a slightly higher peak for less than thirty seconds during orgasm. (The average individual uses 1.4 calories per minute just sitting quietly in a chair.)

Diets aimed at prevention of disease are important. We know a good deal, for example, about diet and the prevention and control of heart disease in middle-aged men. Although middle-aged women are much less prone to heart disease than men, they catch up after age sixty. Therefore preventive diets are important for them as well. The earliest of heart-disease-prevention diets, the Prudent Man's Diet, devised by Dr. Norman Jolliffe in 1957, is still being revised and updated regularly. This balanced, low-calorie diet lowers the amount of saturated fats and cholesterol you eat. It calls for a total of 2,400 calories a day (compared to the American male average of 3,200), with no more than 30 percent fat in the diet, a cholesterol limit of 300 milligrams a day (roughly the amount in one egg), moderate protein, increased complex carbohydrates such as vegetables and fruits, and a reduction of salt. Low-fat recipes and cooking advice can be obtained from local heart associations, or from the American Heart Association, 44 East 23rd Street, New York, N.Y. 10010.

To help inform you more specifically about cholesterol, we list the following information from the National Institutes of Health Consensus Development Conference on Cholesterol (December 1984) and other recent studies:

- The average blood cholesterol for all Americans today is 210 mg. For persons aged forty and over, a cholesterol level of 240–260 mg (per deciliter of blood) indicated moderate risk of heart attack, while those about 260 mg were at high risk.
- Cholesterol levels below 180 in men may increase the risk of colon cancer, so drastic reductions of cholesterol levels may not be wise.
- A specific fraction of high-density-lipoprotein (HDL) cholesterol, called HDL_2, may be protective against heart attack. Recent studies indicate that an extended program of regular aerobic exercise raises HDL_2.

- Fatty fish, such as salmon and mackerel, and monounsaturated fats, such as olive oil, may have cholesterol-lowering effects, according to recent research.
- Nearly all clinical trials of the effects of cholesterol lowering have focused on middle-aged men. We know little about women, children, or the elderly. Some feel the latter two groups should not restrict their cholesterol intake, because of the risk of inadequate nutrients.

GENERAL NUTRITION TIPS

- Go easy on salt to avoid developing high blood pressure.
- Bulk in your diet is important for digestion. Doctors used to prescribe low-residue (limited-bulk) diets for people with bowel problems, but now just the opposite is generally true. Bulk can be obtained from eating fruits and vegetables (complex carbohydrates) like raw celery, apples and carrots, as well as whole-grain breads and cereals. Bran cereal is good. If you want lots of bulk at low cost, buy coarse bran (health food stores usually carry it). Coarse bran tastes like a cross between babies' Pablum and sawdust, but if you consume several teaspoonfuls in between swallows of liquids at each meal or a larger amount on your breakfast cereal daily, you will be taking an important step in promoting good bowel action and preventing diverticulosis, certain kinds of constipation, and other bowel problems. Bran is far better for you than laxatives. The complex carbohydrates mentioned earlier may be even better.
- Try to avoid getting into the habit of taking laxatives, which can in fact induce habitual constipation. As we have noted, a good diet with plenty of bulk and plenty of exercise is the best way to prevent constipation in later life. If you do need an occasional laxative, many doctors feel that milk of magnesia is preferable to mineral oil, which tends to reduce the absorption of fat-soluble vitamins.
- "Indigestion" from eating fried foods may mean gallstones; consult your doctor. Some liver specialists believe that a low-fat diet can help prevent formation of gallstones.
- Gout, arthritis, diabetes, and a number of other diseases, which can directly affect your sex life as well as your general health, may require a special diet prescribed by your doctor.
- Some overweight people, more women than men, have a bumpy kind of fat popularly known as cellulite on their thighs and hips,

which resembles the texture of an orange peel. It can hang from upper arms or droop around the stomach. There are no reliable techniques for getting rid of this bothersome fat, but exercise, diet, and direct vigorous massage of the affected area on a regular basis may help.

- If you tend to eat poorly, are less than knowledgeable about nutrition, or are under stress, take a standard vitamin-and-mineral supplement to obtain the minimum daily requirement. For the average healthy individual a multivitamin should contain no more than 100–150 percent of the U.S. Recommended Daily Allowance (RDA) for any one nutrient.

- Under certain conditions, you may need professional advice about supplementing your diet. Extreme or chronic dieters, alcohol abusers, strict vegetarians, food faddists, heavy smokers, persons on chronic medication, hospitalized surgical or severely ill patients, and persons with severe acute or chronic illness usually have special nutritional needs.

- Anemia may occur when your diet is inadequate in iron and protein. Foods containing iron are lean meats, dark-green leafy vegetables, whole-grain and enriched breads and cereals. The dietary approach is more economical and just as effective as the highly advertised vitamin and mineral preparations. (Remember that anemia should be evaluated by your doctor.)

- Osteoporosis is a common and possibly preventable disorder affecting more than one quarter of all women over forty-five and one fifth of all men over sixty. It is due to a gradual loss of calcium from the bones (accelerated in women by the menopause—which is why osteoporosis is more of a problem for women than for men) so that they become weak, thin, and easily breakable. Wrist and hip fractures result as people grow older, especially among women. Deformities such as a hump on the back may develop. Factors that increase the risk of osteoporosis are high protein and salt intake, cigarette smoking, heavy caffeine and alcohol intake, lack of exercise, and a family history of osteoporosis. White women seem to be more at risk than those of other races.

- Osteoporosis may be slowed and possibly prevented in a proportion of women by nutrition and exercise, although specific recommendations are still under debate. For example, opinions differ on the significance of calcium intake, and some believe an excess of protein in the diet may be even more significant. For those greatly at risk (your doctor can help you evaluate your risk), estrogen replacement therapy currently is considered the most effective treatment. But because of its known risks, such treatment needs to be carefully evaluated by the patient and her doctor (see Chapter 6). Women may be able to help protect themselves through adequate calcium intake—1000 mg before menopause and 1500 mg after it. (The average intake of adult women is 450–500 mg per day—far too low.) About five eight ounce glasses of milk (skim milk is recommended to avoid fat intake) would supply 1500 mg of calcium. If you don't like milk or it does not agree with you, calcium supplements containing carbonate can be taken. One of the cheapest is regular Tums, which has 200 mg of calcium carbonate in each tablet. Many other foods contain calcium: yogurt, hard cheese (especially Parmesan and Swiss), canned salmon and sardines (eat the bones too), kidney and pinto beans, bean curd, oysters, and collard, turnip, and mustard greens. Bone meal and dolomite are not recommended because of possible contamination with lead and other toxic metals and because dolomite is poorly absorbed in the body. Vitamin D is important in helping the absorption of calcium, especially in its active form which is a hormone known as calcitriol. Sources of vitamin D are sunlight, fortified milk, salmon, tuna, and liver. Some experts believe that calcitriol is the critical element in preventing osteoporosis. Studies are under way to determine whether calcitriol hormone therapy may be more effective than large doses of calcium and even estrogen therapy in preventing bone loss.

- Persons with high blood pressure or a tendency to develop kidney stones and ulcers or other digestive disorders may react adversely to high calcium intake. A physician should be consulted. If calcium tablets cause constipation, more fiber in the diet will be needed. Calcium should not be taken in more than the recommended amount of 1000 mg premenopausally or 1500 mg postmenopausally, because of possibly harmful effects from larger doses.

- Physical exercise that puts stress on the long bones of the body is also protective of bone strength. Regular long daily walks, and moderate lifting that involves the whole body, are recommended. Exercises designed to promote good posture are useful.

- Large doses of vitamin E have been recommended for a variety of disorders, including sterility and vascular diseases, and for retarding the aging process, curing impotence, and healing wounds and burns. There is as yet no convincing scientific evidence for these claims. The recommended daily allowance for women is 20–25 IU; for men, 30 IU.

- In general, be prudent about taking over-the-counter medications

that are widely advertised on television and radio; they are sometimes valueless, often costly, and on occasion—especially if you
take them in large quantities or combine them—hazardous.

• You will find that you feel and sleep better if you make your evening
meal relatively light. Breakfast is a good time to eat heartily. Cutting
down on food and alcohol intake before bed is also conducive to
better sex. If you have had a heavy evening meal, it is best to post-
pone sex for a few hours to avoid unnecessary strain on the heart
and other organs.

• It is a common belief that people need fewer calories as they grow
older. One source claims that your body requires 10 percent fewer
calories between ages thirty-five and fifty-five than when you were
under thirty-five; 16 percent fewer between ages fifty-five and
seventy-five; and one percent fewer calories per year for every year
over seventy-five. We are not totally convinced. We suspect that this
theory is based on the fact that many people become less active and
fail to work or exercise their bodies as they grow older, and that
caloric needs are a function of activity and not of age. Some inactivity is of course related to physical ailments, but much more is
simply lack of motivation and inertia. The older you get, the more
temptation you may feel to take it easy. Lack of movement leads to
poor appetite, which in turn leads to fatigue and a vicious cycle.

REST

A rested body enhances sexual desire and improves sexual performance as well as contributing to general health and well-being. Con-
trary to general opinion, in middle age and later you need as much
sleep or more than when you were younger. You may, however,
notice changes in your sleep patterns. Studies show that as they
grow older, people seem to experience less "deep," or "delta," sleep
(the period of restful, restorative, dreamless oblivion) and become
"lighter" sleepers, with more frequent awakenings. All of the sleep
stages, including dreaming, or REM sleep, decrease proportionately
as total sleep time decreases. In addition, depression, anxiety, grief,
loneliness, and lack of exercise can effect sleep patterns and depth
of sleep. Early-morning awakening is more common among the
inactive, the depressed, those who go to bed early, and those who
take frequent catnaps during the day.

Get seven or more hours sleep per night, according to your needs, which vary from person to person. More sleep is needed if you have physical health problems. If possible, take one or more naps or rest breaks during the day.

If insomnia strikes, don't panic. To prepare for sleep, avoid caffeine drinks like coffee, tea, and colas, especially in the afternoon and evening, since caffeine can keep you awake. Decaffeinated coffee is preferable, although some report that even the minimal amount of caffeine it contains can keep them awake. Exercise can have a positive effect on sleep if completed early enough in the day, particularly if it has been performed regularly for at least two months. Exercise should be avoided for two hours before bedtime to avoid insomnia brought about by stimulation of the body. The establishment of simple rituals can also get you psychologically ready for sleep: a warm bath, a well-made, firm, and comfortable bed and pillows, back massage by a partner, reading a book, watching TV, or listening to music. Often warm milk, one glass of wine, a soothing talk with your partner, or a phone call to an understanding friend can comfort you and relax your tensions.

At bedtime your defenses against anxiety, anger, and other emotions are down. If these create persistent troubled sleep or insomnia, psychotherapy or some form of counseling may help. Avoid nonprescription sleep remedies, since they are expensive and largely useless. Eventually your body will become tired enough to sleep by itself. We don't recommend sleeping pills (hypnotics) unless you are in pain or great physical or emotional discomfort, because they can be habit-forming and may cause adverse side effects, including, paradoxically, the perpetuation of insomnia. The use of hypnotics should be evaluated by a physician on an ongoing basis. Prescriptions should not be automatically renewed time after time. Active, pleasurable sexual activity, including masturbation, can be an excellent sleep inducer.

For help with serious sleep disturbances and disorders, contact your physician. You may be able to find specialists in sleep disorders in your area by contacting the Association of Sleep Disorders Center, P.O. Box 2604, Delmar, CA 92014. For example, the Geriatric Medicine Associates, Department of Geriatrics, at Mount Sinai Hospital in New York has a program focused on sleep problems in middle and later life.

SKIN CARE FOR MEN AND WOMEN

Ideally, prevention of skin problems should begin in the early years, but good skin care can help at any time in life. Skin can be damaged by too much sun or wind, and by malnutrition, excess alcohol, disease, depression, drugs, and anxiety. Overexposure to the sun causes more premature aging, particularly in Caucasians, than any other factor. Sunbathing and working or playing out of doors unprotected for long periods of time are the major culprits. Resultant permanent skin damage can affect both the outer and the inner layers of skin, causing loss of water and elasticity, deep wrinkles and grooves. Prolonged exposure to very cold weather, to overheated rooms with minimal humidity, and to air conditioning in warm climates can deplete the moisture in the skin, making it look lined. Electric blankets left on all night can dry the body skin. Various kinds of air pollution can be damaging. Poor nutrition, whether vitamin deficiencies or unbalanced diets, can cause dry, scaly, and inelastic skin. Sagging skin sometimes follows too rapid weight loss. Anxiety, depression, and tension speed up the appearance of aging. Cigarette smoking can cause wrinkles to appear sooner than they normally would, since nicotine narrows the small capillaries and cuts down the supply of blood bringing nourishment and oxygen to the skin.

Even with the best of preventive care, the face begins to acquire noticeable lines and wrinkles around the age of forty. There is a gradual permanent loss of elasticity in both the skin and the underlying tissue. Wrinkles per se should not become an obsessive concern; "looking your age" does not mean looking unattractive. The facial changes of aging are aspects of individuality. But obviously, all of us—even those not enmeshed in the cult of "youth"—want to look our best. Don't waste your money on "wrinkle removers" and other gimmicks "guaranteed" to make you look younger. Anything that keeps the skin moist will help to slow down the appearance of aging.

Here is a simple regimen that can be followed by women and men who want to take care of their skin. Thorough cleansing of the face and neck is important as the first step. Many people can tolerate a mild soap like Ivory if it is used quickly and rinsed off completely. Neutrogena, which is much more expensive, can also be tried. Others may need to use a rinsable or washable cleanser which combines cream and a small amount of soap in lotion form. (Creams and oils used alone are difficult to remove and the skin is never completely cleansed.) After cleansing and a thorough rinsing with warm water, pat the face dry, and while the skin still holds moisture absorbed from the rinse, immediately protect it by applying a light moisturizer by day or a heavier moisturizer at night. Most inexpensive dime-store creams work as well as expensive ones. About once a week, women should rub something rough on the face, such as cleansing grains or inexpensive cornmeal on a wet washcloth. This helps remove the outer layer of dry flaky cells. (Men need not do this since shaving accomplishes the same purpose.) The body itself can also be protected against drying by using a body lotion immediately after a bath or shower, when the skin has absorbed moisture.

Electric facial saunas dry the skin. The face should really not be massaged, but if you enjoy facial massage, never stretch or pull the skin in a downward direction. Various chemical processes and dermabrasion (removal of the tissues of the outer skin layer with a rotating brush) can be dangerous unless done by skilled operators. They are also expensive. Plastic surgery (face-lifts) for both men and women can correct severe skin sagging; but they, too, are expensive and good results last only three to five years. The best skin care is sensible cleansing, good diet, rest, and the avoidance of cigarette smoking and too much sun, wind, or alcohol.

PART TWO
PSYCHOLOGICAL ISSUES

10

THE SECOND LANGUAGE
OF SEX

When people are young and first getting used to sexuality, their sex tends to be urgent and explorative, involved largely with physical pleasure, self-discovery, and in many cases, the conception of children. This is the *first language of sex*. It is biological and instinctive, with wonderfully exciting and energizing potentialities. The process of discovering one's ability to be sexually desirable and sexually effective often becomes a way of asserting independence, strength, prowess, and power. The first language of sex has been much discussed and written about, because it is easy to study and measure—one can tabulate physical response, frequency of contacts, forms of outlet, sexual positions, and physical skills in lovemaking.

But sex is not just a matter of athletics and "production." Some people recognize this early on and simultaneously develop a *second language of sex*, which is emotional and communicative as well as physical. Others learn the second language slowly as they themselves mature. Still others continue largely in the first language—sometimes all their lives, sometimes only until they begin to see its limitations and desire something more.

The second language is largely learned rather than instinctive, and is often vastly underdeveloped since it depends upon the ability to recognize and share feelings in words, actions, and unspoken perceptions, and to achieve a mutual tenderness and thoughtfulness between oneself and another person. It goes far beyond "falling in love," an exhilaration that is notoriously short-lived and short-sighted. In fact, some scientists claim the sensation of falling in love can be explained by an amphetamine-type brain chemical activated by attraction and novelty. In its richest form, the second language becomes highly creative and imaginative, with splendid possibilities for new emotional experiences and attachment. Yet it is a slow-developing art, acquired deliberately and painstakingly through years of experience in giving and receiving.

In the natural flow of events in the life cycle, times will come when you may find yourself reevaluating many areas of your life, including your sexuality. Middle age is the time when people typically begin to take stock of their lives and reassess their work, their personal relationships, their social and spiritual commitments. Such times can be chaotic, generating emotional upsets, divorce, higher risk of alcoholism, and other evidences of stress. But periods of stocktaking can be constructive as well as dangerous. People have the opportunity to alter their lives and even create them anew. A central question is whether there is a satisfactory fit between what people have achieved and what they still wish for. The second language of sex has a good deal to offer you if you want to move in new directions in your personal life. Shared tenderness, warmth, humor, merriment, anger, passion, sorrow, camaraderie, fear—feelings of every conceivable sort—can flow back and forth in a sexual relationship that has matured to this level of development.

Part of the secret of learning the second language lies in learning how to give. Receiving is much easier. It makes few demands. But the habit of only taking deadens the impulse to reciprocate. As Erich Fromm in *The Art of Loving* (1956) has said, "Most people see the problem of love primarily as that of being loved, rather than that of loving, of one's capacity to love." Giving is *not* an endless gift of yourself to others in which you expect nothing in return. Nor is it a marketplace transaction, trading with the expectation of an equal exchange. Healthy giving involves not only the hopeful and human anticipation that something equally good will be returned but also the pleasures inherent in giving, regardless of return. The balance to be struck is chosen by each person and worked out in partnership with others.

The second language implies sensitivity. It means clearing up long-held grudges and old irritations toward your partner and people in general, so your energy is not wasted in negativity. It suggests the possibility of renewing love every day. It requires knowing what pleases your partner and what pleases you. It involves playfulness as well as passion, and talking, laughing, teasing, sharing secrets, reminiscing, telling jokes, making plans, confessing fears and uncertainties, crying—in the privacy of shared companionship. It need not involve the sex act at all.

If boredom creeps into the relationship, both partners need to acknowledge it; it is time to look for or listen to the deeper feelings that each of you has hidden away against the time when the richness of such feelings can be welcome and restorative. You have to resist the pulls of habit. Routines and responsibilities may have dulled the impulse to really talk, and you must fight against succumbing to the temptation to withdraw into your own self-absorbed world. Self-centeredness, wanting sexual and emotional contact only when you are in the mood, without concern for your partner's needs, is guaranteed to produce conflict. Competitiveness based on some fancied level of sexual performance is also deadly.

The second language of sex can be developed by actively trying to learn it. People may struggle throughout their lives to overcome obstacles, earn a living, raise children, assist their elders, and carry out other responsibilities. In so doing, they have literally sacrificed their private lives and individual growth to the process. But fortunately, love and sex are always there to be rediscovered, enhanced, or even appreciated for the very first time, whether you are young, middle-aged, or old. Self-starters have the advantage over those who wait passively for love to strike like lightning.

Midlife and older people have, we believe, a special ability to bring love and sex to new levels of development, literally because they are more experienced. Many people do learn from the experience of their earlier lives. They develop perceptions that are connected with the unique sense of having lived and having struggled to come to terms with life as a cycle from birth to death. A number of these qualities are beautifully suited to the flourishing of the second language. An appreciation of the preciousness of life and the valuing of immediateness can occur as people grow older. What begins to count is the present moment, where once it was the casually expected future. If the developing awareness of the brevity of life leads you to come to terms with your mortality in a mature and healthy way, no longer denying it, you will find you avoid living recklessly, as though you had all the time in the world. The challenge of living as richly as possible in the time you have can be exhilarating.

Elementality—the enjoyment of the elemental things of life—may develop in mid and late life precisely because people become more keenly aware that life is short. Such people may find themselves becoming more adept in separating out the important from the trivial. Responsiveness to nature, human warmth, children, music, beauty in any form, may be heightened. The second half of life is frequently a beginning of greater enjoyment of all the senses—colors, sights, sounds, smells, touch—as one calls into question hectic schedules and complicated social and work demands. In addition to a maturing disillusionment with the more typically young and midlife drives for achievement, possessions, and power, those who have retired have a special advantage in learning to enjoy life. They have much more actual time for developing both relationships with others and their own personalities, especially if they are in reasonably good health.

Willingness to change counts, as well. It is possible to become quite different in middle and in later life from what you were in youth. Obviously, the change can go in positive or negative directions. But the point to remember is that change is possible. You do not need to become locked into any particular mode of behavior at any time of life. Experimentation and learning are possible all along the life cycle, and this holds true for sex and love. Naturally, the more actively you grow, the greater the reservoir of experience and the larger the repertoire you can draw upon in getting along with and loving other people.

But can love and sex really remain interesting and exciting after forty? What about after fifty, or even after sixty or more years of age? We have summarized some of the responses people have given to the question of what sexuality means in the middle and later years:

- *The opportunity for intimacy through the expression of passion, affection, admiration, loyalty, and other emotions.* This can occur in long-term relationships that have steadily grown and developed, in new relationships such as second or third marriages, and in relationships that may have started off badly but improved over the years.
- *An affirmation of one's body and its functioning.* Active sex demonstrates to people that their bodies are capable of working well and providing pleasure. For many people, satisfactory sexual functioning is an important part of their sense that all is well, and helps to maintain high energy, morale, and enthusiasm.
- *A strong sense of self.* Sexuality is one of the ways people achieve a sense of their identity—who they are and their impact on others. Positive reactions from others preserve and enhance self-esteem. Feeling "feminine" or "masculine," whatever meaning these terms have for each individual, is connected with feeling valued as a person regardless of age.
- *A means of self-assertion.* The patterns of self-assertion available when people are young change as they grow older. Children grow up and leave. Work may lose its newness or even its challenge. Personal and social relationships often become far more important as outlets for expressing personality, especially as people move into retirement and leave work relationships behind. Sex can be a valuable means of positive self-assertion. One older man told us, "I feel like a million dollars when I make love even though we are scrimping along on social security. My wife has always made me feel like a great success in bed, and I believe I do the same for her. We've been able to stand a lot of stress in life because of our closeness this way."
- *Protection from anxiety.* The intimacy and the closeness of their sexual relationship can bring security and stability to people's lives, particularly when the outside world threatens them with hazards and losses. Middle-aged couples can support each other as they grapple with the many stresses of parenting, careers, and other responsibilities. An older couple we know described the warmth of their sexual life as "a port in the storm," a place to escape from worry and trouble. A very much older woman, concerned with eventual death, called sex "the ultimate closeness against the night."

Sex and intimacy can serve as an important means of feeling in charge when other elements of one's life feel out of control.

- *The pleasure of being touched or caressed.* This pleasure is often taken for granted until it is absent. Widows, widowers, and divorced persons describe how much they miss the simple pleasure and warmth of physical closeness, of being touched, held, and caressed by someone they care for. Holding and hugging friends, children, and pets offer some compensation but do not replace the special intimacy and feeling of being cared about that can exist in a good relationship or sexual union.

- *A sense of romance.* The courting aspects of sexuality—flowers, soft lights, music, a sense of romantic pursuit, elegance, sentiment, and courtliness—may be highly significant at the same time they give aesthetic pleasure. Romance may continue even when sexual intercourse, for various reasons, ceases. Mr. and Mrs. Denham, a couple in their eighties, described their evenings together. They typically bathe and dress for dinner, she in a long dress, he in a suit and tie. They dine with candlelight and music, listen to music during the evening, hold hands, and enjoy each other's companionship. At bedtime they fall asleep in each other's arms. Often they awaken in the middle of the night and have long, intimate conversations, sleeping late the next morning. Mr. Denham said of his wife, "I fall in love with her every day. My feelings grow stronger when I realize we have only a certain amount of time left."

- *An affirmation of life.* Sexuality can express joy and continued affirmation of life. The quality of one's most intimate relationships is an important measure of whether life is or has been worthwhile. An otherwise successful person may count his life a failure if he has been unable to achieve significant closeness to other persons. Conversely, people with modest accomplishments may feel highly satisfied if they have had fulfilling intimate relationships. Sexual intimacy is only one way of achieving closeness, of course, but it can be an especially profound affirmation of the worthwhileness of life.

- *A continued search for growth and experience.* Many people continue to search throughout their lives for ways to create new excitement and experiences. Some who are dissatisfied with their present lives look for ways to improve what they already have. Others pursue divorce, remarriage, or new relationships in the hope of finding what they are searching for. Many could find this growth and excitement within their present relationships if they could learn some of the skills that would make it possible. Love and sex are twin arts, requiring effort and knowledge. Only in fairy tales do people live happily ever after without working at it. It takes continuous and active effort to master the processes that eradicate emotional distances between yourself and another and to continue to grow and learn.

The middle years set the stage, but perhaps only in the later years can life with its various choices and possibilities have the chance to shape itself into something approximating a human work of art. And perhaps only in later life, when personality reaches its final stages of development, can lovemaking and sex achieve the fullest possible growth. Sex does not merely exist after the middle and later years; it holds the possibility of becoming greater than it ever was.

The special psychology of sex in the second half of life will eventually be better understood than it is now. Then we will comprehend for the first time the full life cycle of love and sexuality—with youth a time for exciting exploration and self-discovery; middle age, for gaining skill, confidence, and discrimination; and old age, for bringing the experience of a lifetime and the unique perspectives of the final years of life to the art of loving one another. We have a great deal yet to learn from those who personally have mastered this complex and wonderful art over years of time.

11
PROBLEMS WITH PARTNERS

CHANGES OVER TIME

After the age of forty, many of the same sexual problems between partners arise as before the forties: differences in levels of sexual interest, disagreements on sexual frequency, the appearance of sexual rebuffs, boredom, and ambivalence about fidelity. But new features are gradually added with the middle years: a change in family responsibilities, with one's parents becoming older and children leaving the home, more complex social and work roles, concern about bodily changes, and more efforts spent on self-care—all of which can intrude on energy and time that earlier were available for leisure and for social and personal relationships. A need for a sense of adventure and novelty may begin to assert itself. Problems can arise if one partner becomes ill or incapacitated.

All of this takes on new significance when we realize that after the age of forty men can expect to live another thirty-four years and women another forty. Growing longevity for greater numbers of people means that time itself becomes a factor in relationships. Does a relationship have endurance? Can it grow and change in positive new directions or does it stagnate and weaken over time? What do the most successful relationships after forty have in common?

Sexual role changes over time can also cause disruptions. One or the other partner may alter his or her level of assertiveness, affecting the original emotional or power balance between the two. Most typically, women gradually become more assertive and men more nurturant as they grow older. This pattern appears to occur in numerous cultures studied. One of the explanations is that it represents a move toward "wholeness" of personality after the cultural and possibly biological emphasis on gender differences in behavior earlier in life, with young men assuming the assertive roles and young women the nurturing ones.

People may also simply grow tired of their usual roles and desperately desire a change. Sexual boredom and apathy are very common among midlife and older couples, who may fall into routine patterns in which they do the same things time after time, year after year, with little imagination in technique or style and a scarcity of zest for creating sexual excitement. The partners eventually may no longer even care for each other. A new partner may seem to bring improvement, but unless the sources of underlying boredom are dealt with, the improvement may prove only temporary after the novelty has worn off.

Interestingly, relationships that were unstable and unsatisfactory earlier in life sometimes improve in the later years, as the children grow up and leave, and the stresses of parenthood and career pass. On the other hand, long-standing problems between partners can worsen as the result of chronic irritation from years of unresolved conflict. Personality and behavior changes may also be unilateral, as one partner begins to move in new directions, leaving the other behind, often angry and hurt.

What can you do if you and your partner are having relationship problems? First talk to each other about the problems—often. It is important to discover the source of the problem and to cooperate with each other in attempting to resolve it. Be prepared for the fact that each of you may refuse to admit your own contribution to the situation and may blame the other. It is difficult to be open and objective about emotional issues. But it is absolutely imperative to realize that what you should be looking for is a solution rather than a culprit. If you find you need help, go together to your physician, or a professional psychotherapist, a counselor, or a member of the clergy. If your partner won't go, go alone. Separation and divorce, the last resort, can be an extremely painful and jolting experience, and efforts should be made to salvage and improve difficult relationships first. Even if separation occurs, you will have learned something about yourself and your partner that may help you understand the past as you prepare for the future.

SPECIFIC SEXUAL PROBLEMS AND SOLUTIONS

Problems in the relationship with one's sexual partner can very quickly affect sexual functioning. An angry, bored, or otherwise unresponsive sexual partner can lead to potency problems for men and sexual disinterest or lack of response for women.

A low sexual interest rather than impotence per se may be a central problem for many men. Dr. Joseph Lo Piccolo of Texas A & M University believes that chronic low sex drive is much more common among men than was previously thought. He describes most of this as psychologically based, ranging from the effects of feeling overwhelmed by life events to fears of intimacy.

Women, according to Dr. Lo Piccolo, are becoming more likely to question male performance and behavior and are often the ones who initiate treatment for the male with low sexual interest. But women themselves may exhibit the symptoms. Called "frigidity," this behavior used to be interpreted as fear and active resistance to sexuality, but now it is more often viewed as low sexual desire and lack of responsiveness.

Although a lack of sexual desire can be a comfortable way of life for some, it is more often troubling to at least one partner. Sex therapists note that a growing proportion of their patients seek help for what is currently called "inhibited sexual desire." Drs. Raul Schiavi and Patricia Schreiner-Engel of Mount Sinai Hospital's Human Sexuality Program in New York City are studying low sexual desire in a growing effort to understand the phenomenon.

Occasional and short-lived lack of sexual desire is commonplace and reversible. But if low sexual desire is long-lasting, it can be one of the most difficult and intractable of sexual symptoms. For those who wish to change, a combination of sex therapy, psychotherapy, and marriage counseling over an extended period of time may prove beneficial.

When sexual desire is present but physical responsiveness is absent, manifested as impotence in men and failure to lubricate and reach orgasm in women, the causes can be a range of emotions from depression, grief, and stress to anxiety, fear, and anger. Sexual response ordinarily returns when the underlying emotions are resolved or improvement occurs. But such psychologically based symptoms, whatever their original emotional cause, can also quickly create performance anxiety and continued sexual problems if people are intimidated, embarrassed, or frightened by changes in their sexual functioning. This is particularly true of men for whom "performance" carries great importance.

The first step in self-treatment is for partners to relax and assume that sexual functioning is likely to improve once the emotional equilibrium is restored. Kindness and consideration toward each other and a lack of psychological pressure are crucial in providing space and time in which to recover. It is important to remember that sexual response cannot be willed. It is most likely to occur when a person is rested, relaxed, in a positive mood, and in good relation with his or her partner.

Physical stimulation, at first involving the body as a whole and later focusing on the genitals, is an important part of arousal. Masters and Johnson initiated a three-stage method of "sensate focus" which is now used by many sex therapists to teach people to relax and slowly move each other into a state of sexual arousal, eventually resulting in sexual climax. The stages are, first, a stepwise nongenital "pleasuring" of one's partner's body by touching and caressing; second, genital touching and caressing without intercourse; and third, nondemanding sexual intercourse where the goal is pleasure rather than performance.

Special techniques are also available to stop or slow premature ejaculation. Occasional and temporary premature ejaculation happens to most men from time to time, when they have had infrequent sex or are unusually aroused. It usually disappears by itself as circumstances change. Persistent premature ejaculation is another matter. It does not tend to develop for the first time in the mid or later years, but usually evolves early on, and it may continue into later life. Fortunately it is subject to treatment. Reassurance is the first step to try, along with making certain there are regular opportunities for sexual outlet. If these efforts are not enough, a highly successful method has been developed—the "squeeze" technique—in which the woman grasps the end of her partner's erect penis where the shaft meets the glans and squeezes strongly with the thumb and first two fingers for several seconds. This causes the man to lose his urge to ejaculate but allows the couple to continue lovemaking. By alternating the squeezing with sex play, a couple may delay ejaculation until they are ready for a climax. The "stop-start" technique, perhaps the most frequent approach used, refers to stopping genital stimulation until the urge to ejaculate disappears—at which time stimulation is resumed again. If these techniques fail to work, psychotherapy can be helpful. In addition, premature ejaculation may become less of a problem as a man grows older, simply because some of the urgency to ejaculate diminishes.

Partners often find it helpful to talk with each other about their sexual feelings. Embarrassment and feelings of awkwardness are common at first. In addition, many couples first assume that they don't have to talk, since sex "comes naturally." But this simply is not accurate. Because people are all different, with unique likes and dislikes, it is naive to assume that our partners can read our minds or know intuitively how to please us. Furthermore, it is often said that sex begins in the brain, by the stimulation of the imagination and by memory of previous sexual experience. Our mind may well be our most sensitive and reliable organ of sensuality.

Begin by discussing your feelings about talking about sex. Then help each other by telling your partner what gives you pleasure. Finally, try in every way possible to do what is pleasurable for each other. You may be surprised at what you don't know about your partner and what you may have been reluctant to admit about yourself. You can also reminisce, talking about your first memories of sex, your early sexual attitudes and those of your family, and perhaps your feelings about what it means to be a man or a woman. Compare notes on what you would most like to change about yourself and about your partner sexually. Be thoughtful and kind about the way you express any dissatisfactions you may feel. Do not hesitate to express your warmth and affection when these are honestly felt.

Some couples share their sexual fantasies with each other. Such fantasies, which are part of most people's sex lives, involve any visual and sexually stimulating images one conjures up. Some people are excited by imagining forbidden or unavailable sex partners, settings or practices. Others bring to mind sexual experiences from the past that have been especially exciting. Some couples make up fantasies for each other. Recently couples have begun reporting the use of videocassette tapes in their home to enhance fantasy and sexual stimulation.

The value of fantasy is that it adds a new dimension to one's sex life as well as acting as a substitute, rather like an auxiliary motor, if something is not going well. People who may be otherwise fond of their partners but not easily aroused by them as years go by report that fantasies, including fantasies of their partners and themselves when they were younger ("fantasy reruns"), can often get things started and help in reaching climax. Fantasy may be used to override a physical disability or distract a person from anxiety or other preoccupations. Mental imagining can be especially useful for persons whose vision is impaired. Since poor vision can interfere with the vital transfer of visual stimuli into sexual arousal, fantasy may be a means of recapturing such stimuli.

So far we have few useful studies about fantasy in mid and later life. It would be interesting, for example, to know whether people usually fantasize themselves and others as younger than their actual ages.

Books on sexuality and emotional relationships can help couples learn more about themselves and each other. It is useful and stimulating to take a fresh look from time to time at what you know about sexuality, and at the current attitudes of society toward sex. We have recommended a number of books on pages 187–88. There are many more, although most of them assume a young and middle-aged readership. Therefore a book such as *Sex: A User's Manual* (G. P. Putnam's Sons, 1981) is unusual in presenting a separate section on sexuality and aging. Films and tapes that are specifically addressed to medical and other aspects of sexuality in the mid and later years are becoming available to both professionals in health care and the public.

Finding the best time for sexual activity can enhance a sexual relationship. Sex exclusively at bedtime is an easy habit to get into over the years, when daytime privacy is hard to come by and the pressures of work and family crowd your days. Yet this may not really be your favorite time. And after the age of forty, it may not be your most energetic period, either. Overstressed and overworked couples, particularly, may need to set aside several evenings a week to make a date with each other to relax and go to bed early, before exhaustion sets in. Some couples sleep first and make love in the morning. Others wake each other in the middle of the night, when both have had some rest. Many men report greater sexual potency after a good night's sleep. Sex in the morning is a favorite time for many older people because they are rested and relaxed. Naps when possible during the day can make for greater vigor in the evening for those who prefer nighttime lovemaking out of choice rather than by default. Experimenting with new times on weekends, holidays, and vacations can be invigorating. When vacations away from home are not possible, take a vacation at home. If you have the house to yourself, take the phone off the hook and let the outside world know you're not available.

Learning how to relax is also a useful skill. A warm bath or shower before sex can relax you in a pleasant manner. Exchanging massages with your partner, turning the lights low and listening to music, can also help you unwind. (Massage courses for couples are now available in many major cities as part of adult education programs.) A *small* glass of an alcoholic beverage can be a tension reliever—we recommend dry white wine or warm Japanese sake. Warm milk, although not the world's sexiest drink, can bring relaxation.

A WORD ABOUT WOMEN: IS INTERCOURSE OVEREMPHASIZED?

There is growing evidence that women have a different view of sexuality from men, placing less importance on the act of sexual intercourse itself and more on the physical cuddling and personal warmth, talking, and sharing that may surround a sexual relationship. As one example, a controversial survey in November 1984 by the advice columnist Ann Landers among her estimated seventy million readers brought ninety thousand responses from women, 72 percent of whom answered yes to the question "Would you be content to be held close and treated tenderly and forget about 'the act'?" Sixty percent of these respondents were over age forty. Some professionals criticized the survey as incomplete and unrepresentative of women; others felt the large response could not be discounted. Landers herself interpreted the findings as evidence of poor communication in many relationships, with couples failing to resolve dissatisfactions that stand in the way of sexual release for both partners. Another view is that the emotional significance of sexual intercourse for men has obscured the strong likelihood that intimacy is more important than intercourse for many women.

However, there is no convincing evidence that women are less interested than men in achieving orgasm and sexual release. But again, many prefer sexual activities other than, or in addition to, intercourse. Female anatomy plays an important role in women's attitudes. Psychoanalyst Mary Jane Sherfey (1973), Masters and Johnson (1970), Helen Kaplan (1983), Shere Hite (in the Hite Report, 1976), and many others report that the majority of women receive their primary sexual satisfaction from clitoral stimulation and that direct or indirect clitoral stimulation is the initial requirement in the production of female orgasm. Because of this, sexual intercourse is often not satisfying unless it involves direct, manual stimulation of the clitoris. (Less than 50 percent of women achieve orgasm regularly through sexual intercourse, yet a much higher proportion are able to experience orgasm through other methods.) Significant numbers of women prefer manual stimulation alone, without intercourse, in order to reach their own orgasm. For them, intercourse may be an important source of physical intimacy with their partner, but by itself it is not the preferred or most reliable source of sexual release. From the evidence available, one would have to conclude that sexual intercourse has been greatly overemphasized as the most satisfying form of sexual activity for women.

The female capacity for multiple orgasms (women have little or no refractory period—the time period before another orgasm is physically possible—after an orgasm) throughout life is also often not recognized or utilized—either because women do not know they have this potential or because men do not take the time or do not learn the skills to stimulate them. Manual caressing, oral-genital stimulation, and the vibrator afford many women the possibility of more than one orgasm during a period of lovemaking. Males must rely on female guidance in learning what is pleasurable to an individual woman and what is not. There is much variation, but by the time many women reach midlife, they are able to describe well their own particular responses and preferences.

SOLO SEX

Self-stimulation, or masturbation, is a common and healthy practice that usually begins in childhood. It is natural for all children to explore their bodies, and most children stimulate themselves sexually unless they are prevented by adults from doing so. There is evidence that self-stimulation is an important preliminary to adult sexuality, enabling people to learn to recognize and satisfy their sexual feelings. The Kinsey studies of 1948–50 found that 92 percent of men and 62 percent of women had masturbated at some time in their life, and indications are that masturbation has increased in women. The 1982 Merck Manual, a highly reputable source of medical information, reports that approximately 97 percent of males and 80 percent of females have masturbated at some point in their lives. The Hite Report of 1976 found that 82 percent of all women masturbate, and all but 5 percent had orgasms while doing so. The evidence seems clear that although masturbation was once seen as a perversion and a cause of mental and physical disease, it is now recognized as a normal sexual activity throughout life.

Self-stimulation provides a sexual outlet for people—unmarried, widowed, or divorced—who do not have partners, as well as for husbands or wives whose partners are ill or away. Some people practice self-stimulation in addition to sexual intercourse, particularly if they prefer sex more frequently than their partner does or enjoy the variety masturbation affords. As described earlier, many women experience more intense and more frequent orgasms through mutual or self-masturbation than during intercourse. Masturbation can continue until very late in life, and has been reported by some men in their nineties. In a recent Consumer Union survey,

66 percent of men and 47 percent of women in their fifties masturbate with some regularity. Over the age of seventy, 43 percent of men and 33 percent of women still masturbate. Some people begin to masturbate for the first time after they grow older, particularly if they have no partner or become too physically incapacitated for intercourse.

Total abstinence from sexual activity over a long period of time can be tension-producing, and may result in potency problems in men and loss of lubrication as well as of vaginal shape in women. It can be beneficial to free yourself from the notion that self-stimulation is unhealthy, immoral, or immature. A source of pleasure to be learned and enjoyed for its own sake, masturbation also resolves sexual tensions, keeps sexual desire alive, is good physical exercise, and helps to preserve sexual functioning in both men and women who have no other outlets. Vibrators can be useful aids in masturbation. Many people have sexual fantasies, which add to the pleasure of self-stimulation.

LIFE CYCLE CHANGES PERTINENT TO SEXUALITY

DIVORCE

Currently 50 percent of first marriages end in divorce. Seventy-five percent of the divorced remarry, most within five years, and 60 percent divorce again. Of these, three fourths marry for the third time. A flattening of the divorce rate in the past five years indicates that we may have stabilized at the current rates of divorce for the present. Some believe that the practical and psychological problems resulting from divorce and serial marriage will become so severe that there will be a trend back to preservation of first or at least second marriages through more skilled premarital and marital counseling (counseling now prevents divorce in only 10–15 percent of cases, and conciliations have even less success) and less accessible divorce. Others see the tendency toward "serial" marriage as natural and inevitable as people live longer, divorce is easier to obtain, and women are more independent financially.

The process of separation and divorce precipitates more couples into professional counseling than any other life crisis, simply because it is so common and so frequently painful. Clearly minor children are highly vulnerable to suffering unless both parents continue to play involved, responsible, and loving parental roles. Current studies show that at younger ages, men tend to have greater psychological adjustment problems after divorce than women, although women have far more economic problems, especially when there are minor children. In the older age groups, women appear to have the greater adjustment problems: Their financial situation is more precarious, many have no work history outside the home, there are fewer men available for companionship and possible remarriage, and socially, older women alone are often seen as not fitting in or, even worse, stereotyped as boring and uninteresting.

The process of separation and divorce can have serious effects on one's belief in oneself as a socially and sexually desirable person, particularly if one's partner initiated the process. The challenge is to build relationships in which the divorced person feels support, social approval, friendship, and possibly a new intimacy with another person. We have outlined some suggestions for doing so later in this chapter.

RETIREMENT

Retirement can bring problems as well as possibilities for enhancing relationships. The sudden onset of twenty-four hours a day of togetherness can be a difficult adjustment to make. Such unremitting intimacy places greater pressure on emotional relationships and brings problems into more acute focus. What may previously have been an occasional irritant can become constant. A struggle for power or simply control over daily activities can become a preoccupation as each partner strives to adjust to the frequent presence of the other. Even if you can work out these struggles, constant togetherness may dismay or disconcert or irritate you. It is essential that you find a balance between shared time and time alone to give each of you elbow room, and that you talk to your partner about your concerns.

Yet retirement has many advantages for couples. They have more time to devote to relationships, and many couples in fact become closer to each other and to other people after retirement. Schedules are also much more flexible, and one or both members of a couple are less likely to find themselves exhausted when the opportunity for intimacy arises.

CHRONIC AND INCAPACITATING ILLNESS

Illness may incapacitate one sexual partner physically and/or mentally but not the other, particularly when there is a substantial age gap between them. Frequently the man develops a serious illness first, leaving the woman without a companion or a sexual partner. Healthy women—especially those who are significantly younger than their husbands—may spend years in a relationship without adult intimacy or sexual contact. Other feelings can complicate the picture. When one partner becomes ill, the other ordinarily reacts with concern and the desire to help. But if the illness becomes chronic, the well partner may be surprised to find himself or herself filled with anger. This may reflect threat of the possible loss of the other; it can also represent overwork and exhaustion or an understandable resentment over missing out on life because of the duties of the nursing role and the incapacities of one's partner. It is important not to feel guilty about such resentments. Face them frankly and secure outside help whenever possible from your relatives, neighbors, friends, or professional homemakers to reduce the burden. Support groups involving people in similar circumstances can be very helpful. It may be necessary to begin to build new friendships to provide a sense of self-worth and companionship.

At other times illness may cause sexual problems but both partners may still desire and are able to have a relationship that involves closeness and a sense of being valued. Intercourse is the form of sexual activity that is most likely to be impaired. Both partners may feel guilty and need to reassure each other that they can develop other satisfying methods to express sexuality. In general, the less goal-oriented (in terms of erections and orgasms) and the more flexible people are, the more likely they are to find ways to enjoy sex and each other.

Partners with ill or disabled mates at home state that it is difficult to routinely bathe, feed, and provide nursing care for a mate and still think of him or her as a sexually desirable person. If sexuality is otherwise viable and important to the couple, a visiting nurse or a home-help attendant, if affordable, should take care of the least aesthetic parts of patient care. A quick return to roles as normal as possible is the ideal. The expression of your feelings to someone you trust or possibly to your partner, accurate information about the physical problems of your mate, involvement in whatever rehabilitation process is feasible, and finding new ways to express caring and sexuality when necessary are all ways to adapt positively.

It is interesting that the knowledge that an illness of one partner may be terminal or fatal sometimes brings an improvement or a heightening of a relationship. Couples report that the certainty or closeness of death causes them to cherish the present moment and to take advantage of the time they have left together. When sexuality is a part of that closeness, such couples should always have the opportunity for privacy and time alone, even if one partner is confined to a hospital or another institution. If they encounter problems in working this out with the institution, many hospitals and nursing homes have a patient representative department or a social work staff which may be available to help.

INSTITUTIONAL LIVING

The 5 percent of persons over sixty-five who live in homes for the aging, nursing homes, chronic-disease hospitals, and other long-term-care institutions are in general denied the opportunity for any private social and sexual life. Visitors are in full view of roommates and staff and can be overheard by them. Even those who have marital partners are seldom able to share conjugal visits, where the patient is afforded a private time and place with his or her spouse.

Intimacies of any kind between unmarried fellow patients, even hugging or kissing or holding hands, are frowned on despite the fact that they are performed by consenting adults. Even persons who, understandably, resort to self-stimulation because they have no other sexual outlet run the risk of being discovered and reprimanded like children.

Most older persons in these situations are reluctant to complain to the management, even though their rights as adults are being seriously infringed on. Ask the administrator of your particular institution to provide whatever privacy you and other patients should have. If you need outside support, ask your relatives, friends, doctor, lawyer, or a member of the clergy to help you in stating your cause. Speak to patients who have a similar complaint and make it a joint project. You can also alert groups that are interested in the problems of older persons, such as local chapters of the Gray Panthers, the Older Women's League, the American Association of Retired Persons, and the National Council of Senior Citizens. Federal regulations issued on June 1, 1978, provide some right to privacy, but only for married couples, and only in nursing homes that participate in federal Medicare and Medicaid programs (more than two thirds do not). These regulations are not being uniformly enforced, but failure to observe them is ground for legal action. For information, write Health Standards and Quality Bureau, Office of Standards and Certification, Health Care Financing Administration, Rockville, MD 20857.

WIDOWHOOD

Widowhood increases with age, but it is not uncommon in the forties. The losses and grieving that are inevitable as we grow older need to be worked through and accepted, in order that the survivor be freed psychologically to resume a full life or shape a new and different one. Losing someone you have loved—spouse, partner, friend, child—usually means shock and then a long, slow journey through grief. Acute grief, with intense mental anguish and remorse, ordinarily lasts a month or two and then begins to lessen. In most cases, grief works itself out in six to eighteen months, unless it is complicated by further loss, stress, or other factors. *Widow shock,* an exaggerated state that can follow the sudden and unexpected death of a partner or occurs when the surviving partner is ill-prepared to handle living alone, leaves the survivor unable to accept death and take up life again. To recover, he or she needs to be encouraged to grieve and should be given assistance in building an active life once more. The open expression of feelings, including crying, is important for both men and women in resolving grief. Sharing one's sadness, anger, resentment, fear, and self-pity with someone helps.

Such *grief work* also involves talking about your sexual feelings. People need to separate out their own identities from the commingling of identities that has occurred in close and long-term relationships. The feeling that "part of me died with him [her]" can then be replaced with the feeling that "I am a person in myself and I am still alive." A man may find himself temporarily impotent, a symptom we call widower's syndrome, which usually clears up if he is encouraged to grieve and find his way through the loss.

Anticipatory grief, during which a person undergoes an extended grief reaction prior to the expected death of the loved one— as happens in the course of a terminal illness—can soften the shock of death. Such grieving may result in a closer relationship with the ill spouse, but there are instances when the grieving person may close himself or herself off, as though the spouse were already dead. When this occurs, outside counseling help may be needed to reestablish the relationship with the dying person.

After the death of a spouse, it is often very difficult for the man or woman who has been widowed to look ahead to a new partner without feelings of guilt or disloyalty to the memory of the dead mate. In *enshrinement,* the survivor keeps things just as they were when the loved one was alive and spends his or her energy revering the memory of the dead person, surrounded by photographs and rooms maintained intact. The survivor believes that to live fully is a betrayal of love or loyalty for the dead. This survival guilt and fear of infidelity leads to emotional stagnation and stands in the way of achieving new relationships. Once the period of mourning is over and the initial shock and grief have abated, you owe it to yourself to become realistic about your need to have a new life of your own. This means the appropriate preservation of your memories without excessive dwelling in the past. The usual cure for enshrinement is to take an active role in getting life moving again. This is an act of will and determination. It can happen only if the individual decides to make it happen. Removing from sight the personal possessions of the deceased will help. It may also be necessary to put away obvious marriage symbols, such as the wedding ring. It is not a betrayal of a past marriage to accept the present and build a future.

If grief and anger over a death continue unchanged for years, something is interfering with the natural healing process of time. Quite often it is unresolved negative feelings toward the dead person, as in an unhappy marriage, or a stubborn refusal to accept fate (an adult temper tantrum) and to take positive steps toward creating a new life. In these cases, professional counseling help may be necessary.

For those age fifty-five or older, the American Association of Retired Persons (AARP) has a Widowed Persons Service in 170 locations nationwide. A volunteer who has gone through the same experience will be sent to talk to the newly widowed person about his or her feelings, and help with problems. Also available is a "Survival Handbook for Widows." Similar services ideally should also be available to younger widowed persons.

HOMOSEXUAL RELATIONSHIPS

Many people, including many homosexuals themselves, particularly men, believe that life becomes increasingly bleak and lonely as the homosexual person grows older. This is by no means inevitably true. Between 5 and 10 percent or more of all Americans are homosexual; many have long-term relationships, are emotionally stable, and see themselves as successful and happy. The stereotype of the lonely, isolated homosexual in the mid and later years applies to those in the minority who have not found a close relationship as they've grown older and who may have difficulty with intimacy. They also may have lost their partner through death. Some believe there are more males than females in this category, partly because males have a shorter life expectancy than females and partly since the male homosexual or gay community places a strong emphasis on youth and physical attractiveness. Lesbians, or female homosexuals, are seen as more likely to form long-term monogamous or serially monogamous relationships with people their own age, to worry less about physical aging, and to be accepted by the young in their communities. (However, women in older age groups are seen as more troubled and ambivalent about their homosexuality per se than are younger lesbian women.)

There is evidence that homosexuals, especially women, are more planful about growing older since they often have no children and have less expectation of family support. Typically, a self-selected network of friends substitutes for family. However, those who have revealed their homosexuality to family members who remain loving and supportive often have both strong kinship and strong friendship ties.

When difficulties, both social and sexual, occur for homosexual couples, they involve many of the same interpersonal problems faced by heterosexual couples. In addition however, they may find themselves isolated in the larger society, with few role models for growing older in a homosexual relationship or as a single person. There can be lack of support when a partner of long standing is ill or dies. Hospitals and other institutions may not recognize the homosexual relationship in terms of visitation privileges and consultation with medical personnel. Discrimination from younger gays can be a problem for men and perhaps to a lesser extent for women. Self-esteem and self-acceptance may have been compromised through years of social oppression and hostility and/or the need for secrecy. And finally, legal rights are often unclear and unprotected; for example, wills can be contested by relatives if belongings are left to a homosexual partner.

Organizations are beginning to form to aid homosexuals as they reach the mid and later years. Social clubs for those over forty exist in some cities. An organization called SAGE (Senior Action in a Gay Environment) in New York City offers a variety of social services to older members and promotes the opportunity for intergenerational support. The National Association of Lesbian and Gay Gerontologists is actively promoting understanding and services for the homosexual community in mid and later life. (For information, write NALGG, 3312 Descosso Drive, Los Angeles, CA 90026.) *A Legal Guide for Lesbian and Gay Couples* by Hayden Curry and Denis Clifford (Nolo Press, 1981) is one of the books that cover the financial aspects of homosexual relationships: living together, owning property, child custody, breaking up, and estate planning. Sample wills and contracts are included.

Specific sexual issues for male homosexuals are currently dominated by the AIDS epidemic, as described in Chapter 4.

FINDING NEW RELATIONSHIPS

As they reach their forties, many people begin to find themselves without partners, either through divorce or, increasingly with age, through widowhood. This is especially true for women because of longer life expectancies and lower rates of remarriage. Seven percent of women aged forty-five to fifty-four are widowed and 12 percent divorced, compared to 1 percent of men widowed and 9 percent divorced. More than half of all women over sixty are widows, as compared to about 15 percent of men. (About 5 percent of women and 8 percent of men over forty never marry.) Finding yourself without a partner is a possibility that increases with time for women and to a lesser extent for men.

Obviously there are differences between the life-styles of those who never married and who created a circle of friends and intimates that substituted for an immediate family, and the majority, who are abruptly separated from a partner by death or divorce and find themselves on their own. The divorced or widowed person is more likely to feel adrift and anxious about taking the necessary steps to form relationships again. Fortunately, by the time people reach middle age, they are likely to have acquired useful social skills and greater knowledge about human behavior.

WHERE DO YOU START?

Initiative is the first requisite. It is up to you to take action, to decide what you want and what you should do about it. This does not mean you must deliberately be searching for a possible partner. You may want no more than opportunities to meet people who are congenial and likely to share your interests. One way to do this is to look for activities that support those interests. You will feel less tense and pressured if you are doing what you like to do. A sense of pleasure and purpose in what you are doing will encourage you to enjoy, learn, give of yourself, and make friends.

SOME PEOPLE WORRY ABOUT ETIQUETTE

If you are not certain about proprieties, follow the golden rule and your own common sense. Many people are still bound by the customs they were taught as youngsters and many of these formalities make no sense today. Women used to be told it was improper to call a man. But if you are interested, you do not have to wait for his invitations; simply behave as you do when you want to get in touch with a friend. He has the option of accepting or refusing, just as you do when a man (or woman) calls you. If he accepts your invitation, a friendship or a relationship may develop or it may not—but you will have taken an initiative that allows you an *active* role in finding new friends and activities.

BUILDING A SOCIAL LIFE

A variety of activities is available to people without partners who want to develop a fuller social life. Among the best opportunities are those afforded through work, because of the many friendships that become available in most work situations. Even if potential partners are not available, you may meet people who can introduce you to others. If you do not have a job or are retired but are interested and able, consider the possibility of seeking part-time work, both for the rewards of work itself and for the opportunities it offers to meet new people under daily and unselfconscious circumstances.

Where you live will affect the number of choices you have for activities that will widen your social circle, but except in quite isolated rural communities, there are more possibilities than you may realize. If you are politically minded, for example, you can volunteer your help at your local political club. Voluntary work for worthwhile causes, social service agencies, nearby hospitals, or schools may provide you with rewarding work, at the same time that it brings you into contact with people who share similar concerns. Those who like to be active and out of doors can join health clubs, hiking and biking clubs, wilderness and nature groups. If you can't find something that fits your particular tastes, consider organizing it yourself. Any special interests can lead to social contacts.

Religious activities are another important way of meeting people. Many churches and synagogues sponsor singles clubs, and some are beginning to expand these to fit the needs of people in the mid and later years. Talk to your clergyman or woman about starting such a group if one does not exist in your locale. If you are the parent of a child or an adolescent, Parents Without Partners clubs can be a source of contacts and of help to you, both as a parent and as a single person.

The travel industry is actively promoting travel for single people of all ages, with special seminars, tips for solo travelers, and special tour packages. Club Med (800-528-3100), the Sierra Club trips (415-981-8634), Smithsonian Associates tours (202-287-3362), Lindblad Travel vacations (booked through travel agents), and Elderhostel programs (Suite 400, 80 Boylston Street, Boston, MA 02116) are popular with single people. Singleworld (booked through travel agents) offers worldwide cruises and tours for those traveling alone. Travel Companion Exchange (516-454-0880) uses computerized listings to help pair single people for all sorts of travel, not just to arrange companions but to avoid the penalty many hotels, tours, and cruises place on single travelers. Travel Mates (619-258-0220) matches traveling singles with members of the opposite sex. The latest wrinkle is the Freeway Singles Clubs, which began in Huntington Beach, California, and have spread to thirty-six states. Single commuters recognize each other by a club decal on their car windows (purchased for a yearly fee of twenty-five to forty dollars), and the clubs forward letters and telephone calls among members after visual encounters and identification by decal on the highway.

Square dancing, folk and ballroom dancing can bring compatible people together. A number of cities have relatively inexpensive public ballrooms—Roseland Dance City is one such in New York. Friendships and romances can begin in such settings; Roseland has a plaque on its wall engraved with the names of married couples who met there.

High school, college, and other reunions offer men and women the chance to renew acquaintance with compatible people whom they knew earlier in life and who are now widowed or divorced themselves. Family reunions and family contacts in general are another way to get in touch with people who may be seeking new relationships; there is a long and honorable tradition, for example, of widows and widowers who are in-laws developing close relationships that end not infrequently in marriage or partnerships at some level.

Commercial singles clubs and computer dating services are growing in popularity, especially for the young and middle-aged. But there is no reason why older people couldn't use them as well. Personal ads, considered slightly sleazy in the 1960s and early '70s, have become popular and even reputable. For a small fee you can dream up a description of yourself and the kind of partner you are looking for and place it in the classified section of a wide variety of newspapers and magazines. Publications ranging from the *Chicago Tribune, New York Magazine,* and the *New York Review of Books* to the *Village Voice* and the *National Review* all accept personal ads.

Your identity is protected by a post office box number unless and until you choose to reveal yourself to a respondent.

Don't overlook born matchmakers among your friends, acquaintances, and colleagues, your children or other family members. Some people have highly developed sensibilities and can be very helpful in finding men or women you would enjoy meeting. But do save yourself time and trouble by picking your matchmakers carefully; look for someone whose judgment you respect and who knows you well.

QUALITIES THAT FOSTER NEW RELATIONSHIPS

It will help you in your first ventures into meeting new people if you remember that the men and women you encounter are as likely to be feeling tentative or somewhat shy as you are. Actually, you will find that what you look for in other people— as companions, as friends, as co-workers, or as intimates—are qualities they seek just as eagerly in you. Warmth and sensitivity to other people's feelings are greatly valued. One can be quiet or lively, according to one's temperament, as long as curiosity and an active mind underlie this temperament. Imagination, responsiveness, and a sense of humor, are welcomed.

Certain personal qualities foster the art of companionship. Most people respond to a sense of vitality and energy. People who are pleasantly assertive (not domineering) have a greater chance of meeting new people and forming rewarding relationships, simply because they do not leave all the initiative up to others.

CAN YOU BE EXPLOITED?

Exploitation occurs in an emotional relationship when someone "uses" someone else without giving much in return. It may not happen often, but it's possible, especially in the older age groups. It is up to you to know what to look out for and how to protect yourself. Some older men (and, far more rarely, women) marry primarily to gain a housekeeper or nurse. The "romance" disappears as soon as the marriage vows are exchanged, and the woman discovers she has been recruited primarily to perform services. It is much wiser, of course, to take time to learn as much as you can about the other person before you decide to marry. The history of his or her relationships with the opposite sex can be illuminating. Most exploiters have a long history of taking advantage of others.

At other times the exploiter may be after money or property. Matrimonial swindles through lonely hearts clubs and correspondence with strangers who claim a romantic interest are notorious. The tipoff comes when the person begins to be inordinately interested in your property, your money, or your will. If you suspect this is happening to you, get to a lawyer, cleric or someone else you can trust, and ask for advice.

SPECIAL PROBLEMS FOR WOMEN

Unattached women, especially those who are widowed or divorced, often find themselves left out of activities that involve couples. Hostesses at dinner parties often feel they must have a man available for each woman guest, couples coming two by two like the creatures on Noah's ark. The hostess may also find the presence of a widow or divorcee uncomfortable, fearing possible competition.

If you are frequently left out socially, one solution is to join with other single people and organize your own activities. Develop a circle of friends in which friendship rather than gender is the key to getting together, and make these times occasions when people of any age or marital status and either sex can enjoy one another's company. Your married friends can also be invited, and in the process may become less inflexible about their own social habits in inviting guests.

If you are a divorced woman, be prepared to have some people see *you* as a failure; they make the conscious or unconscious assumption that the breakup of your marriage was caused by a flaw in you. Talk this over with understanding people who care about you.

Both widows and divorcees find that some men (married or otherwise) assume that women who are sexually experienced are automatically available and willing. Indeed, these men may see themselves as doing you a sexual favor. If this annoys or upsets you, simply tell them so.

SPECIAL PROBLEMS FOR MEN

As a general rule, unattached men have fewer social difficulties. Even those who had not thought themselves socially very desirable in their twenties and thirties may be surprised to find how eagerly accepted and actively pursued they are after age forty and beyond. This is largely because there are fewer men than women and because our society is more accepting of physical aging in men. A man who enjoys relationships with women is likely to have ample opportunity for them. On the other hand, if you are a man who finds it annoying or troubling to be treated like a commodity in short supply, make this clear, or else remove yourself from those situations where this tends to occur.

Uncertainty can be a problem for men. Many men, like many women, are hesitant, shy, or dubious about their ability to handle personal relationships. To find yourself valued as an available man as you reach mid and later life is not automatically reassuring if you doubt your sophistication, skill, or appeal to the opposite sex. Most men have been conditioned to believe that anything short of confident "masculinity" is shameful, a failure of their maleness. Though a woman may have similar problems of self-confidence, society has not pressured her into feeling "unwomanly" as a result. Any man troubled by doubts about his skill in social and sexual situations should know that he has plenty of company, and that this is no reflection on his manliness. He should also remember that most women he meets are not going to measure him against some impossible ideal and judge him a failure. Further, the man who is shy, diffident, or uncertain about his competence will have to make the same effort of will, and exercise the same degree of initiative, that a hesitant woman must undertake. Without this determination, relationships will not just happen for him any more than for her.

AS A RELATIONSHIP DEVELOPS

New anxieties may occur as a relationship progresses to sexual involvement. When men or women doubt their sexual performance, or fear that the person with whom they are involved may be measuring them against the behavior of a previous partner, it will affect sexual ability. It takes an active effort by both concerned to make the present moment satisfying. Memories of past lovemaking should not be allowed to dominate the present. What each of you can give the other should concern you more than anything else. A caring person who offers reassurance to a partner who is feeling uncertain about his or her skill will help restore confidence. Sexual problems with deep roots may require professional help, but the self-doubt that has its roots in shyness and uneasiness about performance— which is much more common—is often alleviated by thoughtfulness and tenderness.

HANDLING REFUSALS, REBUFFS, AND DISAPPOINTMENTS

However confident they may appear on the surface, a great many men and women worry about rebuffs when they initiate or respond to a social opportunity. How can you handle refusals and disappointments? It is natural to feel hurt, but you need not let this feeling persist. Maturity implies accepting the possibility of rejection whenever you involve yourself with others, so be matter-of-fact about it. It is, after all, the other person's right—as it is yours when you are approached. It should not deter you from further involvements. Rejection actually serves a very practical function, by keeping people apart who would probably be unhappy together.

Obviously there will be occasions when the rebuff is rude and takes no account of your feelings. Inevitably, a certain proportion of your social contacts will prove to be unpleasant, and sometimes painful. This is unavoidable in human relationships at any age. The point to remember is that refusals or disappointments do not mean you are a failure as a person. If you are losing confidence and feel you need a fresh perspective on yourself, talk over your experiences with a close friend. Then try again. Draw on the experience you have gained even from the unpleasant event. Take a few chances. Above all, do not waste time berating yourself for what does not work out. Learn to assess wisely the difference between what is your responsibility and what is beyond your control.

MOVING TOO FAST

What if one partner in a newly acquainted couple moves too quickly toward intimacy? Many people dread the thought of the woman who is husband hunting or the man who is aiming for a sexual conquest on the first date. Use your common sense. Don't be afraid to tell the other person if you are feeling pushed. Make an effort to be sensitive to your companion's feelings, especially if you yourself tend to be an impulsive or action-oriented individual. A relationship that is going to be more than merely temporary needs time to build. People must explore each other's feelings and learn more about each other. Decide together what pace to set. Many people are not ready for physical intimacies—much less marriage—until they feel a mutual understanding and affection. An enduring partnership is based on thoughtfulness as well as attraction.

LIVING WITH YOUR CHILDREN: A NOTE FOR OLDER PERSONS

Living with your adult children, as roughly 20 percent of older people do, can put a damper on your social life unless you take steps to prevent it. Don't depend on your children to recognize your needs for privacy. You will have to take the initiative, and discuss this with them frankly. Work out ways of sharing the space available in the home, so that there will be times when you can entertain people privately. Some houses are large enough for you to have your own suite of rooms, which makes a separate social life easier. But most older people will have a bedroom at most, and sometimes even this will have to be shared with another member of the family. If you have your own room and it is a reasonable size, you can furnish it as a combination bedroom–sitting room and entertain your friends there. If small children live in the house, a lock or latch on the door will keep them from running in and out until they learn to knock and enter only on invitation. Your bed can be a couch by day, and you should also have a comfortable chair and other amenities for entertaining. If you must share a bedroom, arrange to have sole use of the room at certain times. There may be difficulties in entertaining privately in the family living or dining room unless you and your family have worked out a practical schedule. It is easier if there is also a recreation room, den, or library. If your resources permit, you might want to help finance the construction of additional space or undertake some remodeling.

It is extremely important that you make your children aware of your desire for privacy *before* you move in with them. Discussing the issue before actual situations arise is more likely to produce results. When it is they who are moving in with you, things are usually a bit easier because you are on your own territory to begin with. The crucial element in living successfully with one's children is to be able to talk openly with them about problems and cooperate in solving them.

AFFAIRS AND LIVING TOGETHER

The number of unmarried men and women of all ages living together as sexual partners has more than tripled since 1970, with nearly two million such households in 1984. Much publicity has been given to this phenomenon as it affects the young and the middle-aged. But less is known about older persons who live together. Perhaps a much larger number live separately but have affairs. The decision may involve deliberate choice, or it may be a necessity. Two people may care deeply for each other but feel that marriage would set limits on an independence they have come to value after a lifetime of responsibility. We have known older men and women who nursed spouses through long chronic illness until death, and who felt that they did not want to enter into another marriage that might put them through the same ordeal. There are also instances in which marriage is not possible. Unhappy marriages have continued for years because one spouse will not agree to divorce, forcing the other to seek a partner outside marriage. In other marriages, one member may have been incapacitated or chronically ill for a long time, leaving the other without a sexual and emotional outlet. Under such circumstances, outside relationships are more likely if the marital couple had an unsatisfying emotional relationship to begin with, or if one partner is mentally impaired or institutionalized. Sometimes the children of a widowed parent object strongly to his or her remarriage and the parent does not wish to cause family conflict.

Economic factors may enter into decisions not to remarry. There may be pension penalties for remarriage. Recent legislation has improved this situation somewhat, but penalties still remain. State Medicaid benefits for the payment of otherwise unmanageable health care costs can also be a barrier to remarriage. If one partner has been receiving Medicaid, marriage would mean suspending that support until the entire savings of the new spouse were used up; only then could Medicaid be resumed. Indeed, there have been cases where husband and wife divorced each other, though continuing to live together, in order for one of them to be eligible for Medicaid.

In general, the decision of whether to marry or simply to live together is a private one, to be reached by each individual couple. There can be many inducements on both sides, including religious attitudes, the reactions of relatives, financial considerations and personal preferences. Couples must find the solution that best suits their circumstances.

THE DEMOGRAPHIC DILEMMA

Until medical science and public health techniques become more successful in bringing greater equality of life expectancy for men versus women, we shall have to tolerate the social consequences of greater numbers of women than men over forty without partners. However, women are adapting in a number of ways: by challenging negative cultural stereotyping against women, both personally and institutionally, through organizations like the Older Women's League and the Gray Panthers; by learning to take the initiative in building friendships and a social life; and by redefining their own sexuality to include a wider range of options for satisfying intimacy and sexual release. Some are developing relationships with younger men. Others have relationships with married men who may be unable or unwilling to leave their marriage. Some sublimate their sexuality by developing absorbing activities that bring them companionship and accomplishment. Homosexual women are in a particularly advantageous spot as they reach midlife and beyond, since partners who are their own age will have the same life expectancy and they move in a world that becomes increasingly female with each decade.

None of this, however, is a wholly satisfying substitute for increasing the life expectancy of men as well as preserving their physical vigor and sexual functioning as they grow older. Fortunately, we are already seeing improvements, with a dramatic drop in deaths from heart disease in the last ten years for both black and white men and, just recently, a drop in white male lung cancer death rates.

12

DATING, REMARRIAGE, AND YOUR CHILDREN

PROBLEMS WITH CHILDREN

Our patient files contain many examples of conflicts between parents and their children that develop when a parent is widowed or divorced and attempts to build a new life through dating and, possibly, remarriage: "My daughter doesn't like my fiancée, and thinks she is only interested in my money." "My son, Jim, feels I'd be a fool to marry Harry, that Harry has always been a ladies' man." "My children think I'm crazy to want a man. I wouldn't dare tell them what I did on my cruise to Jamaica."

A RANGE OF FEELINGS

Not all children create problems. Many are pleased at the thought of their parents' leading full and satisfying lives. Others have realistic worries about practical implications; for example, if the parents are older, the adult children may welcome the remarriage of a father to a somewhat younger woman, because she will be able to nurse him as he grows older, but they may feel threatened if their mother marries an older man, because it will be a burden on her and potentially on them if he falls ill.

For still other children the reactions are entirely emotional. The thought of a parent becoming involved with a new partner can provoke anxiety, threat, jealousy, hurt, anger, or grief. They may be strongly inclined to offer unasked-for advice and even to take over if they feel a parent is making a mistake. Coercion, threats, and angry withdrawal are not uncommon.

There are numerous reasons why children react so negatively, even as adults. Those who never became fully independent psychologically of a parent use that parent to fulfill emotional needs that should be met by their own mates and friends. In these cases, the child acts possessive or personally aggrieved when the parent becomes involved in a romantic relationship. It is not unlike the behavior of a wounded lover. Possibly the parent (perhaps unconsciously) has encouraged an inappropriately close relationship with this child, or other circumstances have kept the child from emancipating himself or herself. Age is not a factor; a child can maintain such a dependency even when married and a parent himself or herself. The best approach to this problem is to let children know, kindly but definitely, that you intend to lead your own life, and encourage the children to do likewise.

Sometimes parents find that their children harbor the ignorance and misinformation about sex in mid and later life that we discussed in earlier chapters. They cling to the parental image only, and do not recognize or want to recognize that Mom or Dad needs love and intimacy just as they do. It is probable that you have encouraged this yourself by overplaying the parent role whenever you were around them. A good antidote is to tell them more about your social interests and to bring your friends and dates home to meet them. You can still retain your privacy, but they should become aware that you feel entitled to emotional and personal commitments. Though they may never be entirely at ease about your right to a sexually satisfying life, they can often be helped to come to terms with its reality.

ENSHRINEMENT

Children sometimes try to preserve the memory of their deceased parent (or a former relationship with a divorced spouse) by the process of enshrinement. They maintain a fierce reverence for the past and want to see nothing changed, so they consider any new relationships a parent may enter into an affront to their other parent. If you are in this situation, you may find yourself accused of selfishness, insensitivity, or disloyalty; and if they succeed in arousing your guilt, you may feel compelled to sever your new relationship. This is a mistake. Your children need to work through their anger and grief at the death (or divorce) that ended their parents' marriage, and to complete this grief work. They are often bound to the past by a mixture of positive and negative feelings, and it is this ambivalence that must be resolved. Talk to them freely about their feelings, listen to their reactions, and try honestly to answer any questions or clarify any confusion that you can. Let them know, also, how you have handled your own feelings about their other parent.

GRIEVANCES AND GRUDGES

Another problem can develop if children hold grievances and grudges against a parent, which they demonstrate by refusing to condone the parent's right to build a new life. Some of these grievances may be lifelong, others recent; some may be misconceptions and misunderstandings of actions toward them, particularly during their childhood, and others may be legitimate. Children may become critical of their parents because their parents were always critical of them. Others remember being harshly punished or humiliated for innocent sexual experiences in childhood; they grew up thinking sex was wrong or shameful, the sex lives of their parents included. If this is your problem, try to begin listening openly to their grievances—it may be difficult. There is a chance that you and your children can develop a new understanding and respect for each other. Be ready to admit where you may have failed, but don't take the blame for everything. They—your children—and your former spouse played their roles too. The point is not to pin down a culprit, find a "bad guy," or allay grievances by making yourself a martyr, but to clarify what happened, why it happened, and whether anything can now be done to build a better relationship. Frank talk itself sometimes heals old wounds. And when it doesn't, *you* decide what choice you are going to make.

THE SPOILED CHILD

Next we must look at a problem that can terrorize a parent—the spoiled child. This is the child who grows up believing himself or herself to be inordinately important and never stops believing it. Every spoiled child has at least one parent who is easily intimidated, over-indulgent, or lax with discipline. A favorite tactic of such a child is to threaten to withdraw love if the parent does not cater to his or her wishes. This tactic is all the more devastating when the child grows to middle age and attains greater power, as the parent becomes older and loses status and authority. If this problem affects you, the sooner you get a grip on the situation, the better. Do not let your son or daughter dictate to you. It isn't good for you and it isn't good for your child. It may be frightening to think of losing this love, but remember that children rarely "divorce" their parents, at least not for long, and particularly if they know basically that you care about them.

Spoiled children have an intuitive understanding of power, since they learned to use it expertly at a very early age. Use power in your turn, to let them know the score. First of all, *keep your hold on your own money and property*. Then start making your own decisions, particularly about your personal life. Get outside author-ity figures to help you if you need them in the initial battles that are bound to come. Your lawyer or cleric, or a respected friend or family member, may be able to support you when you waver, or speak for you if at first you can't speak. You can be heartened by the knowl-edge that spoiled children usually develop respect for people who refuse to be manipulated.

THE WILL-WATCHING CHILD

Finally, we come to a most painful problem, the will-watching child—found particularly in families where there will be an estate after a par-ent's death and where the parent-child relationship is a troubled one. Such a child is forever worrying about his or her share of the estate and casts a cold eye on a potential new mate. A child like this often plants suspicions in the parent's mind that any close friend or prospective mate is only after money. People can be and have been exploited, of course, but if your mind is sound, you should rely on your own judgment and perhaps that of trusted friends or advisers—and *not* on a child with a family reputation for overconcern about money or an inclination to avarice. (If you begin to have any questions about your own judgment, you can seek legal advice to set up a conservatorship. This will protect you, your funds, and your estate.)

What makes a child obsessively concerned about his inheritance? Many things: parental overindulgence, feelings of being unloved, a long-standing family overemphasis on money, lack of training in the pleasure of generosity and sharing with others. Simple selfishness and greed also exist. This is a difficult problem to rectify unless your child is motivated to discover the basis of his or her attitudes toward material possessions. You can try to understand any part you may have played in shaping these attitudes and see what changes in them you can make. But also protect yourself financially and emotionally from capitulating to your child's demands. Your estate is your own to disperse as you see fit. If your son or daughter puts the pressure on, keeping the provisions of your will secret may help. A child capable of maintaining some rationality in this area, however, may be benefited by knowing exactly what you intend to do, so that he or she can learn to live with it. The important thing is to be decisive, and remain unintimidated by veiled or open threats, pressures, and pleadings focused upon your property.

In general, your children's emotional reactions toward your personal life are likely to run deep and require your special attention if you are to avoid unnecessary alienation and hostility. Family councils and heart-to-heart talks can help enormously. But if all else fails, look for professional advice and try to get your children to join you. If they refuse, seek help on your own, but make it clear to your children (and to yourself) that you are working toward their eventual acceptance of your new life.

PREMARITAL LEGAL PLANNING

Premarital legal planning is advisable and often essential. We will focus on only one important form of such planning, the premarital agreement or contract (also called prenuptial or antenuptial agreements, and not to be confused with modern marriage contracts, which stipulate marital duties and are not legally binding; premarital agreements deal only with money and other property.) Alternative forms (trusts, for example) should also be considered, but are beyond the scope of this book. The premarital agreement requires the consultation of a lawyer.

Wealthy people have traditionally used premarital agreements for marriages at any age, in order to protect family estates. Now that people live longer, with more second, late-life marriages and with more extensive estates to dispose of, premarital agreements are increasingly common. Many parents want to leave at least part of their estate directly to their children and are concerned about the effects of remarriage on this intention. If you are planning to remarry and want to make special financial arrangements for the benefit of your children or any other persons, you and your spouse-to-be can work out a premarital agreement. In most states these agreements are a time-honored method for allaying the fears of children through planning one's estate wisely and in their best interests. Resources are kept intact and unavailable to anyone but designated persons. The agreement customarily describes what will *not* be available to the prospective spouse.

To be legally enforceable, such an agreement must be in writing, by reason of the statute of frauds in force in all states. The Uniform Premarital Agreement Act, approved by the American Bar Association in February 1984, and now in the process of being enacted by all fifty states, can be used as a model for a premarital agreement. As a basic agreement acceptable in all states, it is likely to stand up in court.

HOW DOES A PREMARITAL AGREEMENT WORK?

A widow and a widower plan to marry; each has children. The premarital agreement enables them to plan their respective estates in the way that suits them. The advantage to the children lies in the fact that should their parent die, the new spouse will receive an amount less than ordinary under the Statute of Descent and Distributions and the children will receive more. In addition, the children will receive somewhat more than if the parent had died intestate (without a will).

A premarital agreement is different from a will. It is a waiver to the right to a certain miminum claim to a spouse's property at death. A will can be changed at any time without the spouse's knowledge or consent, while a premarital agreement can be amended only with the consent of both parties. It is binding as of the time of the marriage, whereas a will goes into effect only at the time of death. A will can, of course, be changed to give a spouse more and the children less than the premarital agreement stated. But unless the will stipulates this, the spouse cannot lay claim to any more than the premarital agreement provides.

People of modest means may also find premarital agreements useful, since even a properly drawn will does not always protect the rights of children from a previous marriage. An illustration might be the widower of moderate assets with children by his first wife, who had assisted him in earning the money he has accumulated and whose children contributed actively as well. Now he wants to re-marry, and there is some resentment by the children that the new bride will be automatically entitled to one third (or whatever pro-portion is operative in a particular state) of their father's entire estate in the event of his death. If he chooses to do so, the father can decide to contract a premarital agreement that provides something less than one third of the estate for the new wife, with the rest going to children or grandchildren. Even though the financial gain to the children in such a case may be small, emotionally the process may mean a great deal.

COURT CHALLENGES

There are situations where premarital agreements have been chal-lenged, and the courts have in some cases upheld those challenges if fraud was involved or certain formalities had not been observed. The law says that the contracting parties must be in a confidential (fiduciary) relationship to each other, meaning that there must be a good-faith disclosure of assets. For example, the failure of a man to reveal that he has several hundred thousand dollars (he tells his bride-to-be that he has only twenty thousand dollars so that she agrees to take the sum of five thousand dollars in the event of his death) makes the agreement subject to challenge on the basis of fraud.

IN THE EVENT OF SEPARATION OR DIVORCE

Another problem is separation or divorce. Premarital agreements provide for the eventuality of death, and these agreements are expressly recognized in about one fourth of the states by statute and in most of the other states by judicial decision. When the agreement deals not only with the division of property in the event of death but with the possibility of divorce as well, problems may be encountered. For example, many states hold that agreements entered into before marriage to provide for divorce payments in the event of separation are invalid. However, a recent district court of appeals decision (*Burtoff* v. *Burtoff*) upheld this broadening of a premarital agreement as it related to alimony and property settlements.

INFORMING YOUR CHILDREN

How much should you tell your children about your premarital agreement, or the making or changing of your will? Some parents inform each child fully or have their lawyer do so. Others give a general picture but not the specifics. Still others keep everything totally secret. What you do depends on your own judgment. Children may be relieved to have at least a general idea of your intentions. But if privacy about your financial affairs is important to you, you have every right to keep your arrangements to yourself.

13

WHERE TO GO FOR HELP

We have discussed what people can do for themselves to understand and remedy sexual, personal, and social problems. But when such problems persist, outside professional help may be a good idea.

A thorough evaluation is crucial to determining exactly where the problem lies. The first step in any evaluation of serious sexual problems should *always* be a complete medical evaluation (see pp. 109–10), especially after the age of forty or fifty. Physical problems, such as the side effects of medication, can cause serious sexual difficulties by themselves or they can team up with emotional or social problems to create a baffling group of sexual symptoms. Unraveling the medical aspects of sexual problems may be quite simple or terribly complicated, but it cannot be neglected.

FINDING A MEDICAL DOCTOR

How do you find a doctor who is interested and knowledgeable about sex in the middle and later years? Frankly, it may be difficult. Many doctors have not had sex education as part of their medical school training. Those who graduated from medical school before 1961 had no formal training in this area. This has slowly changed, but you will still find that many doctors are surprisingly un-enlightened and are embarrassed to talk about sexual activity. Far too many draw primarily upon their personal sexual philosophy and experience. This is especially true concerning sex in the mid and later years. Physicians may also share the culture's negative attitude toward growing older, so that the older the patient, the less their interest. It is not uncommon for women past fifty to find that their doctor begins to "forget" to do a thorough gynecological exam during a routine physical examination.

THE SPECIAL DOCTOR-PATIENT PROBLEMS OF OLDER PEOPLE

Most doctors have not had systematic training in the general medical problems of older people. This situation is gradually improving and some medical school programs have begun to include geriatrics— the study of old age—in their curricula. But the lack of knowledge and interest remains widespread among practicing physicians. Two national organizations, the American Geriatrics Society (10 Columbus Circle, New York, N.Y. 10019), with a membership of eighteen thousand doctors, and the Gerontological Society's Clinical Medicine Section (1 Dupont Circle, Washington, D.C. 20036), may be able to help you locate doctors in your area who are interested in geriatrics. You can also write the Office of Information of the National Institute on Aging (National Institutes of Health, Bethesda, MD 20205) or the National Institute of Mental Health (National Institutes of Health, Rockville, MD 20857) for a list of persons or clinics specializing in geriatrics and gerontology, arranged by geographical area.

Remember, however, that there is an extremely small percentage of doctors active in this field. It is also true that membership in these organizations does not guarantee competence in the field of aging, and individual doctors who are not specialists in the field may be equally sensitive and knowledgeable in working with older people. An able and understanding general practitioner or internist who takes care of patients of all ages can serve you very well indeed. If you are lucky, your own doctor may be such a person. Some people, of course, feel more comfortable talking about sexual problems with a total stranger, and if this is the case with you, by all means go to a new doctor. The main point is to consult a doctor with whom you feel as relaxed as possible and whom you trust to be both medically competent and generally receptive toward older people.

HOW TO WORK WITH DOCTORS

There are a number of things you should be alert to as you work with doctors:

- Expect the doctor to take a good medical history, which includes a review of the body's systems and functions as well as a history of present and past illnesses. Specifically, the doctor should ask you about any changes you have observed in your genital organs, including in men any bowing of the penis and in women stress incontinence.

- Be aware that not only do diseases affect sexuality, but the proper control of disease may restore good sexual functioning.

- Expect the doctor to take a thorough sexual and marital history as well as a medical history. Questions are likely to include the ways you and your partner feel about sex, its frequency and pleasurability, and any disagreements you may have. The doctor will also explore the impact of attitudes toward sex you may have developed in childhood. You will find it valuable to share with your doctor the history of any sexual experiences you have had with other people. Male patients should be asked if they have problems with urination, and with achieving and holding erections. They should be questioned as to whether they ever have erections as they wake up in the morning. Females should be questioned carefully as to whether they are having any pain during intercourse and any unusual soreness or bleeding.

- The doctor should ask what drugs you are taking, both prescription and over-the-counter, and be able to explain the sexual side effects of each drug. It is sometimes possible to switch to equally effective drugs with fewer sexual side effects.

- If you have had surgery on any sex organs, the doctor should be able to tell you if this is in any way affecting your sexuality. If surgery is planned, learn in advance any possible sexual consequences. Do not be embarrassed to ask specific questions about anything that is troubling you.

- Discuss with your doctor a program of preventive health care. This should include attention to smoking, drinking, nutrition, exercise, rest, stress, and emotional problems.

- Using these questions and the doctor's reactions to you as a guide, and relying as well on your own common sense, if you feel your doctor's examination has been insufficient, talk to him or her openly about your misgivings. As a patient, you are entitled to satisfaction.

- Watch out for doctors who quickly dismiss your sexual concerns by saying: "Well, you *are* over forty (or fifty, or sixty)!" "What do you expect at your age?" "Go home and take a cold shower." "Stop worrying." "Nothing can be done." Persist in your desire for help, and if the doctor continues to be unresponsive, find a new doctor.

- Finally, your doctor should ask if you have any questions.

After the medical examination it should be fairly clear whether physical problems are the sole or, more likely, the partial cause of symptoms of sexual dysfunction and whether medical treatment is indicated. If the examination shows that bodily changes are not involved significantly or at all, then the search for the cause of sexual problems must move to emotional or psychological areas.

PSYCHOLOGICAL HELP: WHO GIVES IT?

Most sexual problems have emotional components, even when the original cause is physical. Some are entirely emotional in origin. Much of what we have said about the competence and inclinations of medical doctors holds true for psychotherapists and counselors. They may be well trained in treating the disorders of early childhood and adolescence, or of early and mid adulthood, but be unaware of and perhaps uninterested in the emotional problems of later life. Therapists are rarely trained in the specialized area of sex after sixty. Finding a therapist for your middle years is relatively straightforward. Finding one for your later years may require a more extensive search.

There are several types of therapy to choose from. Individual psychotherapy means talking with a therapist one-to-one, on a regular basis. Marital counseling involves both you and your spouse.

Couples therapy encompasses unmarried couples as well. Family counseling includes other members of your family. Psychoanalysis is an intensive form of individual psychotherapy centering on Freudian personality theory and requiring several sessions per week. Other forms of intensive therapy with a variety of theoretical viewpoints are available as well. In group psychotherapy, five to ten patients discuss their problems under the guidance of one or two therapists. Sex therapy is a relatively new specialty, which concentrates on specific sexual problems, teaching couples how to relate to each other and make love more effectively.

The background and training of therapists vary greatly. Psychotherapists can be psychiatrists (M.D.s who specialize in psychiatry), psychologists (masters or Ph.D.s in psychology), or social workers (with master's or doctoral degrees in social work). (The term social worker can be confusing since people may define themselves as social workers because of the kind of work they do rather than because of their training. Ask if the social worker has at minimum a master's degree in social work.) Psychoanalysts have had advanced training in the psychoanalytic method. All these fields require a program of formal education and a supervised training period in psychotherapy or casework. All states require physicians to be licensed, and this is beginning to be true for practicing psychologists and social workers as well. Social workers who are certified by the National Association of Social Workers have had a period of professional training and examination beyond the master's degree (you will see the letters ACSW, for Academy of Certified Social Workers, after their name).

In addition to psychotherapists, there are numerous other kinds of counselors. Marriage counselors work with marriage and sex problems. This is a still unregulated field and practitioners range from competent and well-trained professionals to quacks and charlatans. Be careful to investigate the credentials (professional training and experience) of anyone you are considering as a counselor. Pastoral counseling has grown out of the counseling role of the clergy, with individual clerics giving counseling or supervising and training other clergy and lay persons to counsel. Again, the quality of this counseling depends on the training and skills of each individual, since there are no standard requirements for such training in theological schools.

Well-trained sex therapists are usually much more able than other health professionals to evaluate and help resolve specific sexual problems. A general rule is that if you are seeing your family doctor, cleric, etc., regarding sexual problems, resolution should begin to occur in six to eight sessions. If it doesn't, you should seek referral to a specialist in sex therapy. *All About Sex Therapy* by Peter R. Kilmen, M.D., and Katherine H. Mills, M.D. (Plenum Press, 1983), will help answer your questions about how sex therapy works.

Sex therapists have proliferated in recent years. Following Masters and Johnson's important clinical work in the treatment of sexual dysfunction, thousands of practitioners now offer such therapy. Many are untrained or poorly trained. Some are outright frauds. Because this is a new and unregulated field, without an organized structure of qualifications, requirements, examinations, clinical experience, or peer review—and because sexual problems are so susceptible to exploitation by skillful, smooth-talking incompetents—the choice of a sex counselor requires very careful consideration.

FINDING COMPETENT PSYCHOTHERAPISTS, COUNSELORS, AND SEX THERAPISTS

Some sources to check in seeking a therapist are university medical schools and clinical teaching hospitals (many have sex therapy clinics); local medical or psychiatric societies; university schools of social work; community mental health centers; senior centers; local chapters of the National Association of Social Workers (600 Southern Building, Fifteenth and H Streets, N.W., Washington, D.C. 20036); the American Psychological Association, (1200 Seventeenth Street, N.W., Washington, D.C. 20036; direct your inquiries specifically to either the APA's Clinical Psychology Division or the Division of Adult Development and Aging, lest you get lost in one of their many other divisions); the National Association for Mental Health, with 950 chapters in the United States (1800 North Kent Street, Arlington, VA 22209); the Family Service Association of America (44 East 23rd Street, New York, N.Y. 10010) or their member Family Service agencies; and your family doctor and cleric. If you are older, ask specifically for a therapist who will be interested in working with an older person in sex counseling. Ask for at least two names, so you will be able to make a choice. Friends and acquaintances may be able to refer you to professionals who have been helpful to them, as long as you recognize that individual preferences vary considerably.

The American Association for Marriage and Family Therapy (924 West 9th Street, Upland, CA 91786) is pressing for regulation of persons who call themselves marriage counselors and should be able to refer you to someone in your locale, including Canada.

The American Association of Sex Educators, Counselors and Therapists (11 Dupont Circle, N.W., Suite 220, Washington, D.C. 20036), certifies sex counselor–therapists and has a national roster from which names can be obtained. The Society for the Scientific Study of Sex (P.O. Box 29795, Philadelphia, PA 19117) is an international association of researchers, clinicians, and educators. The Society for Sex Therapy and Research (contact Leonore Tiefer, Ph.D., Beth Israel Hospital, Department of Urology, 10 Nathan D. Perlman Place, New York, N.Y. 10003) is a multidiscipline organization whose members must be actively involved in the treatment or clinical study of sexual medicine and therapy. You may also want to write Masters and Johnson for referral to competent sex counselors near you who have been trained by them (William H. Masters, M.D., and Virginia E. Johnson, Reproductive Biology Research Foundation, 4910 Forest Park Boulevard, St. Louis, MO 63108). The Sex Information and Education Council of the United States (SIECUS) (122 East 42nd Street, New York, N.Y. 10017) is an additional source of information and referral.

The cost of therapy varies from free clinics and free counseling, to sliding fees based on income, up to costs, in 1986, of one hundred twenty-five dollars or more per fifty-minute session. Group therapy is usually less costly than individual therapy. Some health insurance plans partially cover costs of psychotherapy. Many do not. Medicare allows only $250 per year for outpatient psychotherapy, and only if it is performed by a psychiatrist. Few insurance programs cover sex therapy per se. But Medicare pays for treatment of sexual dysfunction if the diagnosis can be included under the category of "psychophysiologic genito-urinary disorder" (diagnostic category 305.6 in the Second Edition of the *American Psychiatric Association Diagnostic and Statistical Manual of Mental Disorders* [DSM II]; recently some insurance companies have begun to request DSM III [Third Edition] diagnoses, which are more specific, i.e.,

302.71, 302.72, etc.). It is wise to inform your therapist of this fact, since it may not be widely known.

The amount of time required for evaluating and, if possible, resolving a particular problem varies. Sometimes a single session can be enough. More often a series of weekly sessions is recommended, lasting from several months to more than a year, or in the case of psychoanalysis, a number of years.

WHAT HAPPENS IN PSYCHOTHERAPY?

You cannot literally change the past, obviously, but you can gain perspective about it, change the way you feel about it, break old habits, and acquire new ways of coping effectively. Through talking about and exploring your past patterns, your lifetime habits of living, you may be helped to understand the sources of your sexual problems, lose certain inhibitions, and find new avenues of sexual expression. Therapeutic counseling does not simply dwell on the past, however. You will be discussing the here and now, your present relationships, always looking for your own responsibility for what is happening in your life. You will be asked questions, comments will be made (some may startle you), and suggestions may be proposed. Working out conflicts and going in new directions, therefore, comes about through joint work by you and your therapist on the past and the present. You work together on your private life. The process may remind you of both parenting and teaching. You retain your basic personality, but if successful, you rid yourself of unwelcome symptoms, gain insight and enhanced well-being, and increase your effectiveness in everyday living. Altogether you are likely to feel better about yourself.

How should you act when you go to the therapist? Once again, be frank. Tell him or her whatever is troubling you. There are certain basic things you can require or expect:

- Your therapist needs to be well informed both about the problems of midlife and older people generally and about sexual problems specifically. Don't be afraid to question therapists about their background, training, and general interest in these areas. Evaluate their answers (or failures to answer) in terms of what you know—from this book and from your own experiences—to be important to you.

- The therapist should ask for your sexual, marital, and personal history, and probably will want a medical report from your doctor. A sexual history should include a record of any sexual dysfunction the patient has, its progression, any history of evaluation and treatment, the patient's current level of sexual desire and functioning, and characteristics of the patient's sexual partner.

- You should feel a sense of rapport and comfort with the therapist by the time you have had several sessions. If not, talk over your feelings frankly. If matters do not improve, you may need to consider a different therapist, since rapport and trust are crucial to working effectively on sexual and emotional problems. Do not consider the need to change therapists the result of a flaw in yourself. Each individual's requirements in a relationship as close as that of therapist and patient are different, and intangible but crucial factors like empathy, perception, manner, and attitude are involved in making the right choice. A personality and approach that are right for one person may be all wrong for another. As long as you are candid in your encounters with the therapist, you can trust your perceptions about whether he or she is a good choice for you.

As for your part in therapy, you must learn to:

- Set aside shyness and embarrassment.
- Open your mind and feelings to new ideas and insights.
- Be willing to actively try new directions in your relationships with others.
- Realize that while many things can improve, some things cannot. Once you have decided which is which, with the aid of the therapist, you then can begin to take advantage of those areas where improvement can realistically occur.

WHAT HAPPENS IN SEX THERAPY?

Sex therapy is a unique, usually short-term form of therapy that has evolved over the past twenty years under the leadership of Dr. William Masters and Virginia Johnson of St. Louis. This method is particularly effective for the rapid treatment of problems like premature ejaculation, vaginal spasm, failure to achieve orgasm, and some forms of impotence. It is more difficult, but not impossible, to treat low or absent sexual desire or lack of pleasure in sex. The original Masters and Johnson techniques required a male and female therapist for each couple, a two-week stay in a hotel near the treatment center (so the couple was isolated and could concentrate on therapy), and daily therapy sessions. Patients were given two years of follow-up assistance from therapists available twenty-four hours a day, usually by telephone, for no extra charge. Most sex therapists have now modified this so that couples can remain in their own communities and homes and have therapy once or twice a week for about fourteen sessions. Educational counseling about sex, improving communication between a couple, and carrying out "pleasuring exercises" are all part of treatment. Therapists may use movies or slides in their teaching, as well as group therapy. Couples with marital problems that go beyond their sexual difficulties are encouraged to obtain marital counseling and/or individual psychotherapy. Individuals who are not part of a couple are also accepted for sex therapy.

Even sexual problems that have existed for many years have the possibility of resolution. This is true whether you are middle-aged or older. Therefore, whether your sexual problems are new or long-term, as long as they are troubling to you, you owe it to yourself to see what can be done to resolve them. In many cases you can be rewarded with good results.

14
WHAT DO WE SEE FOR THE FUTURE?

We believe that medical research on sexuality will move in the following directions:

- There will be further improvements in longevity and vitality throughout life, as we learn more about what goes wrong with the body and how we can better cure and prevent the diseases of the mid and later years.
- The life-expectancy differences between men and women will begin to shrink for both positive and negative reasons. Positively, we will learn more about controlling diseases that now kill men earlier than women. We may also learn from observation of women what it is they do that helps them live longer. Negatively, women may lose some of their life-expectancy edge over men as more and more of them adopt heretofore predominantly male habits like smoking and excess use of alcohol. Nevertheless it is clear that women do have a genetic advantage over men, so that some differences in life expectancy will remain.
- The adverse effects of drugs, including alcohol and recreational

drugs, on sexuality will become better understood medically and more widely known among the general public.

- We will see further study of the natural course of menopause, greater clarification of the benefits and risks of estrogen therapy, and an intensive search for safe means of relief for women suffering from symptoms of estrogen deficiency.
- The neurological and hormonal aspects of impotence will become better understood and more treatable.
- Better penile prostheses will be developed, along with improved techniques for surgical treatment for men with vascular problems of the penis.
- We will learn much more about the effects of disease and disability on sexuality and what can be done about them. Much of what has been thought to be aging effects on sexuality will turn out to be subtle disease and injury, and therefore will be treatable or preventable.

Social and psychological research will begin to focus more extensively on the existing and largely unexplored territory of the middle and especially the later years:

- We will learn about the patterns and variations of sexuality and relationships over the life cycle.
- Studies of the sexual effects of changes in psychological dominance as people age will give us greater clues about the psychology of relationships. For example, most current studies show women increasing in dominance as they grow older, while men give up or gradually lose dominance.
- We will learn more about the skills and traits of those people who manage to change and grow throughout life and who remain interested and enthusiastic about themselves, their personal endeavors, and their emotional involvements with others.
- The nature of sexual fantasy in the mid and later years will be explored. Do people fantasize themselves as they are or as they were in the past? Does the nature of what is erotic change over the course of life?
- We will develop a greater understanding of the unique qualities of sexuality in the middle and later years—the effects of experience, of a more highly developed and complex personality, and of the passage of time.

The above is as much a personal wish list as it is a prediction of the future. Nevertheless, it is all within the realm of possibility and probability as we learn to appreciate the intriguing complexity of the body and personality over time.

GLOSSARY

Androgen Any of the *steroid** hormones produced by the adrenal glands and the *testes* that develop and maintain masculine characteristics; *testosterone* is the best known.

Anus The opening from the lower bowel (colon) through which solid waste is passed.

Atrophy A wasting away or diminution in size of a cell, tissue, organ, part, or body.

Bartholin's glands Two small, roundish bodies, one on each side of the vaginal opening. Although they produce mucus in sexual excitement, they are not the primary source of vaginal lubrication during intercourse.

Benign prostatic hypertrophy (BPH) Noncancerous enlargement of the *prostate* gland that occurs in the middle and later years.

Bladder The distendable elastic sac that serves as a receptacle and place of storage for the urine.

* Words italicized are defined elsewhere in the Glossary.

Cervix   The part of the *uterus*, sometimes called the neck, which protrudes into the *vagina*.

Circumcision   Surgical removal of the foreskin, a loose fold of skin that surrounds the head of the *penis*.

Climateric   See **Menopause**.

Climax   See **Orgasm**.

Clitoris   A small, erectile organ at the upper end of the *vulva*, homologous with the *penis*, and a significant focus of sexual excitement and *orgasm* in the woman.

Coitus   Copulation, coition, sexual intercourse.

Cowper's glands   A pair of small glands lying alongside and discharging into the male *urethra*. They contribute lubrication during sexual activity.

Cystitis   Inflammation of the urinary bladder.

Dyspareunia   The occurrence of pain in the sexual act, usually experienced in the female vaginal area.

Ejaculation   The forceful emission of the seminal fluid at *orgasm*.

Ejaculatory impotence   Inability to ejaculate.

Erogenous zones   Sensitive areas of the body, such as the mouth, lips, buttocks, breasts, and genital areas, which are important in sexual arousal.

Estrogen   One of the active female hormones produced by the *ovaries* and the adrenal glands, which has a profound effect on the generative organs and breasts.

Fallopian tube   The tube that leads from each *ovary* into the *uterus;* after *ovulation* the ovum travels through the tube on its way to the *uterus* and fertilization takes place in the tube.

Flashes (or flushes), hot   A symptom associated with the hormonal changes during *menopause*, caused by a sudden rapid dilation of blood vessels.

Foreplay   Sexual acts which precede intercourse during which the partners stimulate each other by kissing, touching, and caressing.

Frigidity   An imprecise term applied to various aspects of female sexual inadequacy: (1) popularly, abnormal lack of desire, or coldness; (2) inability to achieve an *orgasm* through intercourse; (3) inability to achieve orgasm by any means; (4) any other level of sexual response considered unsatisfactory by the woman or her partner.

Genital area   The area which contains the external genital organs such as the *vulva* in the female and the *penis* in the male.

Genitalia   The reproductive organs, especially the external organs.

Hormones   Chemical substances produced in the ductless (endocrine) glands of the body and discharged directly into the blood stream. They have specific effects upon the activity of a certain organ or organs.

Sexual hormones regulate the entire reproductive cycle. (The body produces many nonsexual hormones as well.)

Hormone therapy The medical use of supplementary hormones (other than or in addition to those produced by the endocrine glands) for treatment of diseases and deficiencies.

Impotence Lack of erectile power in the male *penis*, which prevents copulation.

Labia Two rounded folds of tissue that form the outer boundaries of the external genitals in the female.

Libido Sexual desire.

Mastectomy Surgical removal of a breast.

Masturbation Stimulation of the sex organs, usually to *orgasm*, through manual or mechanical means.

Medical specialties regarding sex:

    Endocrinology The functions and diseases of the ductless (endocrine) glands.

    Gynecology The diseases, reproductive functions, organs, and endocrinology of females.

    Urology The functions, organs, and diseases of the urinary system in males and females and of the reproductive system in males.

Menopause The time of life for the human female, usually between the ages of 45 and 55, which is marked by the cessation of *menstruation* and *ovulation*. It may be gradual or sudden, and it can last from three months to three years, or even longer. It marks the end of the childbearing potential.

Menstruation The periodic discharge of the body fluid (menses) from the *uterus* through the vagina, occurring normally about once a month.

Nocturnal emission Ejaculation of *semen* at night while asleep; often called a wet dream.

Oral-genital sex Forms of stimulation of the genitalia by the mouth:

    Cunnilingus Stimulation of vulva (especially the clitoris and labia) by the partner's mouth and tongue.

    Fellatio Stimulation of the penis by the partner's mouth and tongue.

Orchidectomy (orchiectomy) Removal of one or both *testes;* castration.

Orgasm The culmination of the sex act. There is a feeling of sudden, intense pleasure accompanied by an abrupt increase in pulse rate and blood pressure. Involuntary spasms of pelvic muscles cause relief of sexual tension with vaginal contractions in the female and *ejaculation* by the male. It lasts up to ten seconds.

Ovaries The two major reproductive glands of the female, in which the ova (eggs) are formed and *estrogen*, or female hormones, are produced.

Ovulation   The process in which a mature egg is discharged by an *ovary* for possible fertilization.

Papanicolaou smear (Pap smear) test   A simple test to determine the presence of cancer of the *uterus* by analyzing cells taken from the *cervix* or *vagina*.

Penis   The male organ of sexual intercourse.

Perineum   (1) The internal portion of the body in the pelvis occupied by urogenital passages and the rectum; (2) the internal and external region between the *scrotum* and *anus* in the man, and the *vulva* and *anus* in the woman.

Pituitary gland   An endocrine gland consisting of three lobes, located at the base of the brain. The body's "master gland," it controls the other endocrine glands and influences growth, metabolism and maturation.

Potency   Sexual capacity for intercourse; the ability to achieve and sustain erection. Applied only to the male.

Premature ejaculation   Almost instant *ejaculation* (within 3 seconds) upon entry of the *penis* into the *vagina*.

Prostate   A walnut-sized body, partly muscular and partly glandular, which surrounds the base of the urethra in the male. It secretes a milky fluid which is discharged into the *urethra* at the time of emission of *semen*.

Prostatectomy   Surgical removal of part or all of the *prostate*. There are three types, depending upon the anatomical approach: (1) transurethral (TUR); (2) suprapubic (or retropubic); and (3) perineal.

Prostatism, prostatitis   Inflammation or congestion in the *prostate*.

Refractory period   See **Sexual response cycle.**

Replacement therapy   See **Hormone therapy.**

Scrotum   The sac containing the *testes*.

Semen   The whitish fluid containing sperm, which is discharged in *ejaculation*.

Sensuality   The wider aspect of *sexuality;* the involvement of all the physical senses that enhance and express one's sexuality.

Sex   (1) Urge for and (2) act of sexual union.

Sex hormones   See **Hormones.** Sexual hormones regulate the entire reproductive cycle.

Sexual dysfunction   A general term for different varieties and degrees of unsatisfying sexual response and performance.

Sexual fantasies   Vivid and excitatory imaginings about sex; healthy and common in both sexes.

Sexual response cycle   The physical changes that occur in the body during sexual excitement and orgasm. It includes four phases: (1) the excitement or erotic-arousal phase during foreplay; (2) the **intromission** or plateau phase; (3) the **orgasmic** or climax phase; and (4) the **resolution** or recovery phase. The time required for the completion of recovery—the time required before the first phase can be successfully initiated again—is called the **refractory** period. The refractory period is more critical to the male.

Sexuality The emotional and physical responsiveness to sexual stimuli. Also, one's sexual identity, role and perception; one's femininity; one's masculinity.

Sperm Spermatozoa, the male reproductive cells, produced by the *testes* and discharged during intercourse into the *vagina*.

Sterility The incapacity to reproduce sexually; infertility.

Steroids A class of chemical substances that includes the *sex hormones*.

Testes (testicles) The two male reproductive glands, located in the cavity of the *scrotum*, the source of spermatozoa and the androgens.

Testosterone A male hormone (an *androgen*), a *steroid*, produced by the testes.

Thyroid gland The gland partially surrounding the windpipe (trachea) in the neck whose function is to supply hormones which adjust the metabolism of the body.

Urethra The passage or canal in the *penis* through which the male discharges both urine and *sperm*. In women the passage through which urine passes.

Urethritis Inflammation of the *urethra*.

Urogenital system The organs that serve the functions of urination, sexual activity, and procreation.

Uterus (womb) The hollow muscular organ in the female in which the embryo and fetus develop to maturity.

Vagina The tube or sheath leading from the *uterus* to the *vulva* at the exterior of the body. It receives the *penis* during intercourse.

Vaginitis Inflammation of the *vagina*.

Vas deferens The duct from each *testicle* that carries *sperm* to the *penis*.

Venereal disease Any disease which is transmitted during sexual intercourse.

Virility Masculine vigor, including potency (from which it must be distinguished), sexual prowess (skill), sexual frequency, and attractiveness.

Vulva The external female genitalia, including the *labia, clitoris,* and the outer *vagina*.

Womb See Uterus.

BIBLIOGRAPHY

Almvig, Chris. *The Invisible Minority: Aging and Lesbianism.* Utica, N.Y.: Department of Gerontology, University of Syracuse at Utica, 1982.

Berger, Raymond M. *Gay and Gray: The Older Homosexual Man.* Champaign, IL: University of Illinois Press, 1982.

Brecher, Edward M., and the Editors of Consumer Reports Books. *Love, Sex and Aging.* Boston: Little, Brown, 1984.

Butler, Robert N., and Myrna I. Lewis. *Sex After Sixty: A Guide for Men and Women for Their Later Years.* New York: Harper & Row, 1977.

Comfort, Alex. *The Joy of Sex.* New York: Crown, 1972.

Comfort, Alex, ed. *Sexual Consequences of Disability.* Philadelphia: Stickley, 1978.

Fromm, Erich. *The Art of Loving.* New York: Harper & Row, 1956.

Gay, Peter. *The Bourgeois Experience: Victoria to Freud.* Vol. 1, *Education of the Senses.* New York: Oxford University Press, 1984.

Hite, Shere. *The Hite Report: A Nationwide Study on Female Sexuality.* New York: Dell, 1976.

Kaplan, Helen S. *The Evaluation of Sexual Disorder: Psychological and Medical Aspects.* New York: Bruner/Mazel, 1983.

Kinsey, Alfred C., Wardell Pomeroy, and Clyde E. Martin. *Sexual Behavior in the Human Male.* Philadelphia: W.B. Saunders, 1948.

Kinsey, Alfred C., Wardell Pomeroy, Clyde E. Martin, and Paul M. Gebhard. *Sexual Behavior in the Human Female.* Philadelphia: W.B. Saunders, 1955.

Masters, William H., and Virginia E. Johnson. *Human Sexual Response.* Boston: Little, Brown, 1966.

————. *Human Sexual Inadequacy.* Boston: Little, Brown, 1970.

Rothman, Ellen. *Hands and Hearts: A History of Courtship in America.* New York: Basic Books, 1984.

Sherfey, Mary J. *The Nature and Evolution of Female Sexuality.* New York: World, 1973.

Starr, Bernard D., and Marcella B. Weiner. *The Starr-Weiner Report on Sex and Sexuality in the Mature Years.* Briarcliff Manor, N.Y.: Stein and Day, 1981.

Weg, Ruth B., ed. *Sexuality in the Later Years.* Orlando, FL: Academic Press, 1983.

The only medical journal that covers clinical and psychosocial components of sexuality and family life is *Medical Aspects of Sexuality,* 300 Harmon Meadow Boulevard, Secaucus, N. J. 07094. It is published monthly.

INDEX

189

ABOUT THE AUTHORS

ROBERT N. BUTLER

Dr. Robert N. Butler, a Pulitzer Prize winner, has been Brookdale Professor and chairman of the Gerald and May Ellen Ritter Department of Geriatrics and Adult Development of Mount Sinai Medical Center in New York City since 1982.

As chairman of the first Department of Geriatrics in an American medical school, Dr. Butler is a national leader in improving the quality of life for older people. He came to Mount Sinai from the National Institutes of Health, where he created the National Institute on Aging in 1976 and served as its first director. Under his leadership, the need for federal funding for research in gerontology gained recognition. One of his achievements was the establishment of research programs for the study of Alzheimer's disease.

A prolific writer, he won the Pulitzer Prize in 1976 for his book

Why Survive? Being Old in America. *He is a member of the Institute of Medicine of the National Academy of Sciences, is a founding Fellow of the American Geriatrics Society, and has served as a consultant to the United States Senate Special Committee on Aging, the National Institute of Mental Health, Commonwealth Fund, and numerous other organizations.*

MYRNA LEWIS

Myrna I. Lewis is a psychotherapist, social worker, and gerontologist with a special interest in the social and health issues of midlife and older women. She is a full-time member of the faculty of the Mount Sinai School of Medicine in New York City (Department of Community Medicine). She has a part-time private psychotherapy practice in which she specializes in working with men who are presidents of their own companies or chief executive officers. She is also currently a part-time doctoral student in social work at Columbia University.

Ms. Lewis has co-authored two books with Dr. Robert Butler, Aging and Mental Health: Positive Psychosocial and Biomedical Approaches *and* Sex After Sixty: A Guide for Men and Women for Their Later Years, *as well as a number of professional and popular articles. She makes regular appearances on radio and TV on the subjects of aging and on women's issues and is a frequent lecturer to professional and public groups.*

Butler and Lewis are married to each other and are the "geriatric" parents (ages fifty-two and forty-one at the time of delivery) of a daughter who is now six years old. Butler has three grown daughters from a previous marriage. Both authors were raised on farms (New Jersey and Minnesota) and now live in Manhattan.